raw
ingredients

John
Smith
Edwards

Practical Lessons from
a culinary Life

Acknowledgments

<u>Inside Cover art</u>: Shannon Thek
<u>Chapter Sketches</u>: Lauryn Edwards
<u>Poetic Contributions</u>: Nyomi Edwards
<u>Foreword</u>: Sheri Nicholls
<u>Creative Team</u>: Stephen Prier/Chloe Edwards

I dedicate this book to the following:

~God, to whom I am eternally grateful for second and third chances

~Chloe, Lauryn and Nyomi (the three brilliant beams of light that God has blessed me with), may you always shine

~Sheri, for your patience and support

MENU

FOREWORD

I have read *Raw Ingredients* twice now. As I continue to serve along side John in juvenile detention center ministry, the book has enriched my understanding of him and his journey. I am better able to understand his passion for serving troubled youth. When you read *Raw Ingredients*, you may go through a variety of emotions. Throughout its pages you will at times experience laughter, humility, amazement, heartbrokenness and encouragement. It is good to know that the Lord is with us always. Whether we realize it right off the bat, or we learn it the long and hard way through life's challenges. We all have our own road to travel. Whether you choose to dance, paint, sing, play piano, or cook: whatever your passion, *Raw Ingredients* will inspire you, knowing that Christ is always with you through life's struggles!

~Sheri Nicholls~

INTRODUCTION

Life can really be a tough road sometimes. As a Christian who worked in the very volatile restaurant industry for sixteen years, I can attest to that. Moving through the pages of this book, you'll notice it's organized in the format of a menu. More specifically, it resembles what's known as a tasting menu. In high-end restaurants you will often see a tasting menu. It will be comprised of several small "tasting-size" items. It's not uncommon to enjoy five to seven courses, or even more. The idea is to allow the diner to more thoroughly experience the chef's range of abilities. The miniature size of each course helps you to enjoy a broad spectrum of dishes without feeling like you need to be carted out in a wheel barrow when the meal is over.

Each phase of my life is represented in the form of a menu item. Just as a tasting menu contains various small offerings, my culinary career consisted of many jobs, none of which was longer than four years. Over a period of sixteen years, that's a lot of jobs! I was everything from a fast food cook, to a dishwasher at a family style restaurant, to a cook in a four-star establishment, to the executive chef of a country club, and many points in between.

Though the book covers many areas of my life, it is deeply rooted in cooking. On a surface level, many people may wonder what it's really like to be a chef. Hopefully, this book will be a useful tool for those that find culinary arts intriguing and wish to learn more about how professionals do what they do. However, as with lots of endeavors, there are so many metaphors for life that can be drawn from the act of cooking itself. At certain moments, this book may seem heavy on culinary concepts but I promise you, it's just a set-up to segue into a practical life lesson. You can meander along with me, as we dissect the spiritual, mental and emotional aspects of each season of my life. We'll explore how those areas affected my cooking, and how my cooking in turn, affected all of those areas.

One of my goals has been to shed some light on the life of a common chef, who never entered the public arena of star chef status. More importantly though, I want to approach the life of a common *man* from a Christian point of view, uncovering familiar struggles that so many of us may go through. I aim to break down religious barriers that we often times place ourselves behind which only separate us from each other and from God. I also want to encourage those individuals, chefs and non-chefs, who may find this life very difficult to navigate. To let you know you are not alone and that with God's grace all things are possible.

Throughout the book we unearth numerous life lessons along the way. We journey from my youth, through young adulthood and into my middle-age years. The entire writing process has actually caused me to learn and grow. There are so many things I didn't realize about my life until I got into a place of true reflection. *Raw Ingredients* has been a huge eye-opener for me. You would think that I would have already known all of these things about my life, since I lived it. Hind sight is 20/20 and I just didn't understand as much, until I went back in time all these years later. As I traveled through the memories, some lessons were so straight forward they were an instant shot of spiritual adrenaline. Others, however, made me have to put on my big boy pants. These are the tough ones; the spiritual cud that requires some chewing, pondering, partial digestion, and eventual revisiting. As you journey through the pages of this book, I pray that you find life's answers. More importantly, I pray you uncover life's most precious questions.

"The best cook is he who can take the smallest and seemingly most unimportant ingredients and create a fine dish."

~NME

Chapter 1:

~ *AMUSE BOUCHE* ~

OH, to savor the promises of God, that they may whet the palate of our passions and cause us to strive with earnestness through the meal of life. I have had an interesting and rewarding culinary career that has taken me to many different types of venues. I have been everything from a fast food cook to the executive chef of a country club. At the age of 16, I began cooking and did so until about the age of 32. Currently, I am working in the health care field as a Physical Therapist Assistant.

My dream, however, is to open a fine dining restaurant that is Holy Spirit-led. I aim to hire people that the world would say are on the "fringes" of society, people who need hope restored in their lives. Also, the food will be affordable. I believe, and have always believed, that fine cuisine can be offered at a reasonable price. I want to make my cooking accessible to as many people as possible, not the other way around, as so many fine dining establishments have done. It is my intention to make it an *inclusive* experience, not an *exclusive* experience. This by the way, isn't a new or cutting-edge concept. It is the same model Christ uses for His Church... *inclusion* over *exclusion*.

Before we dive into the depths of a culinary life though, I want to first bring you up to speed concerning my life prior to cooking. I was born in Jacksonville, Florida on August 17, 1973. I didn't have a middle name, so I was born John Smith. Now talk about a run-of-the-mill name. There was nothing special about that name, other than the fact that is was uncommonly common. My parents were very poor and very sickly. I had two older brothers, a younger brother, and a baby sister. Due to chronic health issues and economic hardship, my parents made the difficult decision to put the three oldest children into the foster care system. My two older brothers went to live with a military couple stationed in Mayport, which is the Naval base just outside of Jacksonville. I went to stay with a foster mom in another part of the city. Periodically, we had parent/child visits downtown where our biological parents were able to spend time with us and our foster parents.

During one particular visit we were all there. My biological dad and mom with my younger brother and our infant sister. My older two brothers were there with their foster parents. Last but not least I was also there. I was happy and enjoying the company of my siblings. Apparently, that visit made a big impression on me. Later, the social worker called my older brothers' foster parents and told them that ever since that visit with the whole family, I had become withdrawn and wasn't eating anything. She asked them if she could bring me to their home, for a trial period, and see how it went. She thought I may do better if I were with siblings. It worked and I fit right in. Through the course of time, they adopted two of us. As our new parents, they wanted us to keep our biological last name within our new names. My name was now John Smith Edwards and the rest, as they say, is history.

Being in the military, we moved around a lot. In 1980, when I was seven years old, we moved to England. While stationed there, we visited Scotland and Germany. We later moved to Gautier (Go-SHAY), Mississippi. Whew! Talk about a culture shock! Imagine two little black boys with mild British accents living in Mississippi in 1983. Oh yeah, did I mention our dad was African-American and our mom was Scottish? That's right. Mr. and Mrs. Edwards were a mixed couple, who had met years earlier when he was stationed in Scotland. I'm sure we were an anomaly to those small town Mississippians.

After only six months, we then moved to Virginia Beach, Virginia, where the Edwards clan grew when we adopted a biracial baby sister. Finally, in 1986, we moved here to Tampa, Florida, where our dad soon retired from the U.S. Navy at the rank of Chief. By the time I was thirteen years old, God had taken me to places that I would have never dreamed of going. Not bad for a little boy from Jacksonville with a super common name.

Unfortunately, all along the way I carried with me a knack for getting into mischief. I was that one who didn't know how to stay *out* of trouble. I had a huge problem with lying. My mom would say, "John, I don't know why you try to lie, you're terrible at it. I always know when you're not telling the truth." My dad was the final authority. If he had to get involved, you knew you were in trouble. My parents were great parents, but they were very old school, even for our day. Let's put it this way, we had to pay some physical consequences when we did wrong. It was "on like Donkey Kong" when we messed up. But the Bible says that foolishness is bound in the heart of a child. I was definitely that foolish child. One would think that if you knew the dire consequences of your actions ahead of time then why do it? Well, that's what it means to be foolish. Proverbs 22:3 puts it plainly: "The wise foresee danger ahead and avoid it, but fools keep going and suffer the consequences." Thank God for His grace and mercy continually in my life.

The first chapter of my culinary career can be characterized as the *Amuse Bouche* (amooz-boosh), which literally translated from French, means 'mouth amuser'. In the kitchen, its usually referred to as simply the *Amuse*. It is a small, complimentary tasting of one or two bites that precedes the meal. The *Amuse* is meant to awaken the diner's palate with a short burst of flavor, texture and aroma. It also puts the diner on the same page as the chef by introducing you to his or her general cuisine, while giving a glimpse into the chef's current culinary travels. Many times it incorporates humble, leftover ingredients that would otherwise have been thrown away by the average unknowing cook. However, in the hands of a talented and insightful chef, they are transformed into an elegant prelude to an unforgettable dining experience. Though life can get to the place where it seems like a bunch of unworthy raggedy circumstances, we have a living God who wants to transform those scraps into a savory life that will be a blessing to many. The book of Zechariah 4:10 says, "Do not despise these small beginnings, because the Lord rejoices to see the work begin..." Well, my beginnings were definitely humble and at times very amusing. During this first and very transient phase of my career, I worked in the fast food industry. It allowed me to experience many "short bursts" of flavor, texture, and aroma that piqued my culinary interest.

I remember the summer of '89. I was fifteen years old and I was riding high on the inspiration of a memory from earlier that summer. During that summer, my future high school opened the gymnasium each day for all of the budding athletes to show off their skills on the court and in the weight room. I only weighed a buck fifty, so the weight room was not going to be my stomping ground. But the hardwood would be.

At 5'10", I was fairly short. But what I lacked in height, I made up in hustle. My wiry frame allowed me to exploit every seam in the defense with quickness and agility. Each day there gathered the same core of guys (and occasional girls) to "thump the rock" as my dad would put it. One guy in particular stood out to me; not because of what he did *on* the court, but for what he did *off* the court. Every afternoon at a certain time he would end his last game with, "I can't play another game 'cause I gotta go to work." As cheesy as it sounds, I was truly inspired by this fifteen year-old who was a member of the working class. I thought it sounded so cool to be able to say, "I gotta go to work," especially at the age of fifteen. He was my age, and if he could do it, so could I.

I soon mustered some determination and put on my nice dress slacks, a crisp white shirt, tie, and dress shoes. Then, I hopped on my bike and rode the 20 minutes to McDonald's on the corner of Bloomingdale Avenue and Bell Shoales Road. Once I got there, I parked my bike and calmly went into the bathroom to gather myself (so as not to look totally crazy after that brisk ride in the blistering Florida summer sun). I filled out an application and I got an immediate interview. The manager told me that she couldn't hire me yet because I was only fifteen, but that I could come back when I was sixteen, and she would hire me. It sounded like an empty promise, and I was just naïve enough to take her up on that proposition, seeing as how my birthday was only about a month away.

On August 17, 1989 I walked back into that same McDonald's and asked to speak with the same manager. I must have said something like, "Hi, yes... my name is John Edwards and you interviewed me earlier this summer and told me to come back when I was sixteen and you would hire me. Well, today is my sixteenth birthday." She actually kept to her word and took me through a second interview (I believe she still had my application on file) and hired me. I left McDonald's that day feeling like a man…a sixteen year-old, employed man! Thus a career was born.

About three weeks later, football tryouts would begin for the varsity squad and I intended to "be in that number." For this reason, my dad said that I could only work on Saturdays and Sundays, so as not to get overwhelmed with juggling school, football, and work. I was scheduled to work the opening shift, which was from 6am to 2pm on both days, every weekend.

The first morning, I awoke to my alarm going off at 5:20am. I had my time perfectly budgeted. I would spend twenty minutes getting ready, and I already knew it would take another twenty minutes to ride my bike there. Ah yes, the days of youngsters actually riding a bike to work in the wee morning hours. It's very reminiscent of the old paper route! My first day, I was assigned to work with a very tiny and very hard working Asian lady, whom we simply, yet affectionately, called "Yap." I have no idea what her real name was, but she was very sweet and as reliable as the day is long. Through her broken English and many hand gestures, she showed me the ropes, and we went on to make a great team.

The single most memorable food lesson I got from her was how to make biscuits. Yes, I said biscuits. In those days McDonald's made the biscuits from scratch, or at least what we would nowadays call semi-homemade. We started with a bagged product which contained flour and a leavening agent with probably small chunks of lard and salt. We poured it into the large mixer and added buttermilk. My friend Yap taught me things like how long to mix the dough, and on what speed; how it should look, and that it's done when it starts to pull away from the sides of the bowl and form a ball. She showed me how tacky it should feel, and how to flour the counter and roll the dough out on it. Yap also showed me how to dip the dough cutter in flour and rapidly cut the biscuits, tray them, and then bake them. She taught me what color they should be when they come out of the oven, and the magic that occurred as we brushed them with melted butter and they turned from a pale, starchy color, to a glossy, golden brown. I learned the value in seeing something through from raw ingredients to finished product. I'm not sure how they do it now, but it is a very interesting thing to be able to say that I learned how to make biscuits at McDonald's. Who knew I would learn scratch cooking at a fast food establishment? I have since found that we can learn many lessons from the most unlikely sources. God is everywhere, just waiting to empower us with His wisdom.

I learned various lessons over the course of that year, like how to work fast, yet neatly and efficiently (the whole point of fast food!). I also learned how to be a productive member of a team. Perhaps the most valuable lesson was knowing what it meant to be "in the weeds." This is a term we kitchen workers use to denote being buried under a lot of work with serious time constraints. The ultimate scenario for a fast food worker would be having the drive-thru line wrapped around the building, and the lobby full of patrons. The challenge was *not* total avoidance of the weeds. I quickly realized that getting into a tight spot happens to all of us, at one time or another. The true test rather, was in learning to focus on the goal at hand; to break it down into smaller tasks, and not allow myself to get overwhelmed by the bleakness of the situation. McDonald's has very specific ways of doing everything. Some may criticize it and say it is "cookie cutter" style where there is no individuality of thought. It does, however, teach you how to "trust the process." I didn't know Christ at that point of my life, but He knew me, and was teaching me even then. We can sometimes find ourselves in situations that seem absolutely hopeless. These are moments when we want to leave the process we've learned and do things our way. But God always has our back. It was gratifying to learn how to "dig myself out" without becoming hopelessly lost beneath a sea of demands. Phillipians 4:13 tells us, "I can do all things through Christ who strengthens me."

As promising as this part of my life sounds, it was the start of very serious problems for me. From the start of school that year I was constantly in trouble at home. My parents were very, very good parents but I just could not seem to stay in their good graces. The problem was that I had a hard time following their rules because I didn't respect the way they enforced them. When we are young, we tend to form ideologies and philosophies that seem right at the time; the problem is there is greater wisdom beyond our years. I was extremely strong-willed, or hard-headed to be more accurate. Now mix that with a set of parents that were very old school.

My Dad had just retired as a Navy Chief and was now working as a detention deputy Downtown in the Morgan Street Jail. He was very intelligent, very firm, and very intimidating. My mom was this five-foot-nothing, Scottish fireball. I only lasted through the first two games of the football season and my parents made me quit because I couldn't keep my priorities straight. I was devastated, and to add insult to injury they made me go to school and tell the head coach myself. Talk about humbling! I remember thinking that was the toughest day of my life. Little did I know, I would come to see much tougher times.

Over the next two years, my sometimes self-induced stress factor would go up to a ten. During that Sophomore year, I ramped up a habit I had started back in ninth grade...sneaking out of the house. I used to put myself through so much torture. I would climb out of my bedroom window, rendezvous with other kids, stay out all night into the early morning, and still get up for school. Now, this is where the suburbs are different from urban neighborhoods. This is the kind of nonsense we were doing. We weren't stealing other people's cars. Instead we were joy riding in my mom's minivan that I figured out how to get out of the garage while everyone was sleeping. I was even able to use the garage door opener, put the van in neutral, roll it out of the garage, close the garage, start the van and drive off. Criminality takes a lot of ingenuity to devise a plan, and a lot of guts to pull it off.

What an awesome world this would be if we could learn to use all that energy for God's purposes. I developed a saying later when I was in my thirties; "Life is a force, use it for good." If joy riding in my mom's stolen van wasn't bad enough, we were going around smashing mailboxes with a baseball bat. What a moronic thing to do, but that's what happens when you choose the way of hard-headedness. Needless to say, we eventually got caught and the police called our parents. That night/early morning I got beaten with a vengeance. Whew my dad was hot!

During my junior and senior years I went on to work at Little Caesar's Pizza and Winn Dixie Supermarket. By this time, I was seventeen years old and my relationship with my parents had completely deteriorated. I didn't have a relationship with Christ either. My parents were good parents who taught us right from wrong, but we weren't raised in church. I had gone through my entire childhood and into young adulthood not knowing Christ. I had become a loner who, to this day, still struggles with making friends and just hanging out with others. All the way through those years I felt uncomfortable in my own skin. My parents did the best they could, as they did all they knew to do. Unfortunately, our best isn't good enough without Christ.

I had pushed my parents so far that they told me that when I turned eighteen, I was out. My eighteenth birthday was going to fall about a week before my senior year of high school would start. Being the obstinate child that I was, I moved out with my best friend during the summer following my junior year just prior to my eighteenth birthday. I figured I was going to show them what time it was. The kitchen in our new efficiency apartment would have been stocked full of nice plates, glasses and silverware, too, but my mom had thrown them all out prior to my great escape.

You see, my friend and I had been going on what we called "shopping sprees." That was our term for shop-lifting. Oh yes, we had racked-up all kinds of merchandise. We would have been set if my mom hadn't been snooping in my bedroom closet one day (again, good parenting). She found the 20-gallon trash bag full of brand new items. She was livid! That was the last straw. It was time for me to fly the coop.

During the first nine weeks of my senior school year, I walked to school every day and left early for work. I was in OJT (On the Job Training). This was a program where if you were ahead in your credits you could opt to take one less class and get out of school early each day and go to work. It also counted toward your graduation credits. The program was part of DCT (Diversified Cooperative Training). I was actually nominated by my peers as the president of our school's chapter of DCT which was considered a service club. At the district meeting I was runner-up in an election for District President. I was voted Vice President in a run-off between the two of us that had garnered the most votes. Again, so much potential hampered by so much obstinate behavior.

Each day I walked from school to Winn Dixie, where I had to work as many hours as possible because my best friend had moved back home with his parents, so the bills were on me. But hey, I was living the life! I remember always being hungry in school because I couldn't afford to pay for lunch. I was always broke. I eventually had to move back home. It turned out things at home hadn't been as bad as they could have been; which we usually don't realize until they actually get as bad as they could be. This stent at home didn't last very long though. A day came later that school year that must have completely broken my mom's heart. School had just let out for the day and I didn't get on the bus to go home. I was at wit's end. I couldn't stomach going home. I wandered around the campus for a while, pondering my decision. After a short time, I had gotten my resolve. I went to a pay phone by the band room (yes we still had to use pay phones then...no cell phones!). I dialed home and when my mom answered the phone, I told her I just couldn't do it; I couldn't come home anymore. Then I hung up the phone. I don't even remember if I gave her a chance to respond before hanging up. Because I was eighteen I was considered an adult, so my parents couldn't report me as a runaway. I was gone again. This time I was completely on my own. Or so I thought. God was actually keeping his hand on my life; I just didn't know it yet.

I had no apartment this time. A friend, who would end up proving to be my best friend, begged his parents to let me stay with them. But his dad wasn't having any part of it, which I can understand. My friend ended up giving me a pair of shorts, a jean jacket and sneakers. I would usually sleep very lightly for a few hours on a park bench at the local shopping center during the wee hours each night. I always felt half-awake because I had to have a heightened sense of awareness of everything around me. I was still going to school, for what it was worth, although I wasn't really engaged.

It was now March of 1992, and we were entering Spring. In Florida, our early Spring is very bipolar, as the weather is pretty cold overnight and very hot during the day. I was burning-up each afternoon while walking around after school wearing my shorts, t-shirt, and carrying my jean jacket. Then I would freeze at night, as I donned the jacket while trying to stay warm. One night in particular, the freezing wind and overnight low temperatures were getting to be too much. I took shelter behind a Citgo gas station. As I nestled behind the building, a female worker came out to throw the trash in the dumpster while carrying out her closing duties. She was startled by my presence and called the police. When they came, they gave me a trespass warning. Because I was eighteen, they had no legal obligation to help me. I told them my story but they couldn't do anything about it. I either needed to go home to my parents' house or find somewhere else to crash for the night. They said that if I came back, and the people called them back out, then I would be arrested.

With warning in hand, I left the premises. I walked and contemplated for a couple more hours trying to stay warm. After a couple of hours of enduring the ever-dropping temperature and freezing wind, I made a decision. I headed back to the Citgo. I had reached a place of such desperation that I figured, having "three hots and a cot" was worth gaining a criminal record as an adult offender. I went back to the store and saw an older woman inside prepping to open. I knocked on the door and yelled through the crack between the two doors, "Do you have anything I can have to eat!" She immediately got scared and called the police. The same two officers showed up that came the first time. When they arrived they were like, "Hey man we told you we were going to have to arrest you if they called us out again. Why would you come back?"

There are times when you are going through something and others around you just can't relate to your struggle. There are also times when it seems God is nowhere to be found. These are the times, I now realize, that God was the closest, making sure my life was spared. He was allowing me to go through this ordeal without cracking under the pressure and going crazy. He also kept me safe. No, I wasn't going to be doing "hard time", but County Jail would be hard enough for a military brat that grew up in the suburbs. I had a tumult of feelings on the inside. On the one hand, I was relieved to be heading for a warm bed, security, and hot food. But on the other hand, I was actually just a scared eighteen-year old young man. After being processed in central booking at Orient Road Jail, I was issued my "county blues." At almost daybreak I was finally able to lay my head on a real pillow in a real bed and get some sleep.

Over the next two weeks, I probably drank more coffee than I ever had before, and have since then. I soon went to "TV Court", as they called it. We were brought into a court room within the jail where the judge was on a closed-circuit TV monitor from downtown. It was my arraignment. I entered a plea of guilty and was sentenced on the spot, because I waived my right to a trial. He sentenced me to fourteen days incarceration. This was my fourteenth day already, so he credited me with "Time Served" and said I was free to go. Again, God was looking out for me. He made it so that my parents, who knew where I was because my dad was a sheriff deputy, didn't come and bail me out. If I had gotten out on bail then I would have had "papers", which means you aren't finished with the system yet. You have "papers" stipulating a future court date, which will produce court fees and most likely probation. Staying in jail for the full two weeks actually was a blessing, because I had served enough time already, and I was scot-free when I got out...no papers!

I got released at about 11:00pm and began walking down Orient Road toward State Road 60. As I headed down SR 60, a police officer pulled up and began questioning me. Again, God was looking out for me. I told her I had actually just gotten released from Orient Road and she let me get in the squad car and gave me a ride. When we got to my parents' street I told her which house. She dropped me off in the middle of the street and I walked toward the front door of the house. As I walked I saw her drive off. I stayed in the shadow of the front entrance way until I saw she was gone. Then I turned around and headed to the back of the neighborhood. This was a relatively new subdivision, so they were still building and selling houses in the back section. I found one of the newly built houses with the back-sliding glass door unlocked. I went in, locked myself in the bathroom, laid on the floor and went to sleep.

Again, I didn't realize it at the time, but God was providing for me. That cop didn't bother to wait and watch me go inside my parents' house when she dropped me off. There was also no alarm on that empty house and the sliding glass door was unlocked. There is no God like our God. Some may say that it wasn't God because I was doing something illegal by sneaking into that empty house. The thing is God knew I wasn't going to stay at my parents' house that night. He also knew my intentions. I had no plans on vandalizing the property or stealing fixtures or something crazy. He wasn't looking at the action, but rather the situation behind the action. He was yet again providing for his child. This house was built for a time such as this. There was plenty of time to host a family that would pay to live in this house. In the meantime, it was sitting empty, waiting to receive this hard-headed child that was in need of a break. God's grace continually astounds me.

The next morning I got up and washed up in the sink (yep, the water and electricity were on). Then I headed off to school. I was still doing the school thing though it was a moot point by now. When I got there I went to class and the teacher told me I needed to go and see the Assistant Dean of Students. The Assistant Dean told me that the county informed them I was incarcerated because I was a student enrolled in that school. He advised me to drop-out and enroll in night school and get my GED. He said I would be finished before the regular school year ended, if I kept on pace with my work. The problem was that our school didn't offer night school, so I would have to find a way to Brandon High School. It was the closest school that offered night classes. It was about 10 miles away and I didn't have a car. I was going to fail that semester because incarceration was considered an unexcused absence. I had zeros in every class for two weeks. Our meeting was on a Friday, and he told me I could think about it over the weekend, and let him know my decision on that following Monday. I remember heading to class after our conversation and I ran into a friend who was running an errand for her teacher. I told her my situation and her advice to me still haunts me to this day. She begged me, "John, don't do it. Don't do it. Don't drop-out, you won't go back and finish." As I play it back in my mind it seems like I'm watching a movie about someone else's life and I want to yell at the screen, "Take her advice man, don't drop-out!" Sadly, when Monday had come, I walked into his office and told him I was going to drop-out and enroll in night school. I went to a couple of classes, but it was too difficult bumming rides everyday to and from, so I stopped going after less than a week. By this time, my parents had gotten a divorce and I moved back in with my mom.

It was now April of 1992, and I was an eighteen-year-old high school dropout. Obviously college wasn't an option (so I thought at the time). I was, however, being very heavily recruited by the school of hard knocks. I landed a job at Kentucky Fried Chicken, where I would further hone my biscuit making skills. It was a franchised location owned by a family who also owned two other locations. They had a Chief Operating Officer, whose name now escapes me. I just remember he was a man of few words and always wore a serious look on his face. One day, he came in and performed his usual inspection of things. How was the customer service? Was the dining room and kitchen clean? How was the quality of the food product? At some point during his visit he came into the kitchen and asked, "Who made those biscuits in the warmer?" I knew it was me so I sheepishly answered, "I did, sir." He then replied, "They're excellent... good job." That one interaction gave me a big boost of confidence. It may seem small, but that little bit of encouragement went a long way in my young and impressionable mind.

Each day, I took it as a personal challenge to make biscuits that not only the COO would be proud of, but ones of which I was proud. I was starting to learn the hard and fast rules of kitchen life, like the fact that a little (or a lot!) of hard work and patience does pay off. Moreover, there was another lesson in that experience that has since become a guiding principle for me, which was to do my best and stand by my work. I also learned the flip side of this lesson during the daily rigors of biscuit making, chicken frying, and digging myself out of the weeds. In standing by my best work, I had to also be willing to receive criticism that would help my best become even better.

By the end of that summer, I started dating a girl that my best friend had wanted me to meet. Her name was Lisa, and she was a senior at my old high school that coming year. I ended up taking her to the homecoming dance, complete with limo and all. The limo wasn't because I was extra cool or anything. It was born more out of necessity. Not only did I not have a car, I didn't even have a driver's license. We dated for a while, and then on one of the worst days possible I broke up with her…New Year's Eve! I know; what a terrible thing to do. I honestly don't know what was going through my head. I have no idea why it *had* to be that night.

It was during this season that my life would be changed forever. My friend's dad finally allowed me to stay with them, as I was now working and showing myself willing to become a productive member of society. I believe his mom had been heavily in prayer on my behalf the entire time. They were a Christian family, and one day when my friend and I were chilling in his room, he asked me a pivotal question. He asked me if I knew Jesus Christ. I said no. The truth is I had no idea who he even was. I only knew he was a religious figure in history. I actually thought he wasn't real, just a mythical character in the world of fanatical religion. One of the stipulations to my living with them was that I had to attend church with them every Sunday. Through the course of time, I eventually answered the alter call and accepted Jesus Christ as my Lord and savior. I didn't know the magnitude of my decision. I just remember feeling like I had been doing a lot of wrong, and I was supposed to admit my wrong to Jesus and start obeying Him. I had no clue what it even meant to be a Christian. The stage was now set for me to witness the miracles in my life. He had been doing it all along, but now my eyes were open to actually see His goodness all around me. God had me right where he wanted me. But make no mistake. I was in for many more seasons of knuckle-headedness. Eternal salvation is instant; earthly salvation is a life-long process.

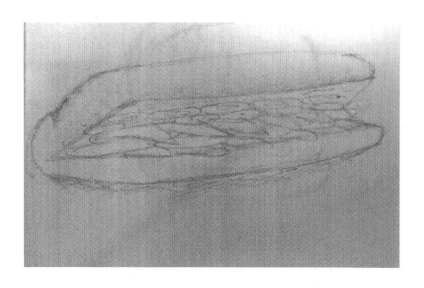

"When a man becomes weary of striving, he must be fed a kindly helping of bread and meat, and alas… he must be pushed some more."

JSE

Chapter 2:

~ ALL AMERICAN GRINDER ~

The second chapter of my culinary career could be characterized by the term "grinder." This comes from the New England, Italian-American vernacular for a long sandwich that's hard to chew, because of the Italian bread piled high with meats and cheese. Nowadays, these thick sandwiches are often cut into smaller pieces and served on a platter as hors d'oeuvres or appetizers. If the task of the *amuse* was to pique our interest, then the appetizer is to whet the appetite. It is the appetizer's job to satiate the now engaged salivary glands by introducing some light faire to the palate. This phase is where I moved from fast food cook to short order cook. It is also the time when I learned the five-day-a-week (often six-day-a-week) "grind."

I was a 19-year old high school drop-out hustling to survive, and life was upon me. I was entering the "All American Grinder." My mom had subsequently allowed me to move back in with her, after her divorce from my dad. Once again, that didn't last long. She came home from being out of town one morning to find I had a female in bed with me. She was incensed. I was on the move once more. It was time to get to work and pay some bills. My time as a fast food cook had gotten my attention, and now I was ready to take on the "turn and burn."

After leaving mom's place, I moved to an area just east of Tampa called Thonotosassa (pronounced Thuh-no-tuh-sas-uh). It is a Seminole-Creek word derived from *thlonoto* and *sasse* meaning "flint is there." Apparently there was an abundance of flint found in the area when it was settled between 1812 and 1820. Fitting, since the job I held while living there was the flint that sparked the flames of my culinary interest.

It was around January of 1994, and I had moved to the area and was living with the family of an ex-girlfriend who had recently joined the Navy. It was actually that same girl my mom had caught me with a while earlier. Her parents were gracious people who enjoyed helping struggling young people like myself by giving us a place to stay while we got on our feet. It was extremely altruistic of them, considering I wasn't even dating their daughter anymore. God had brought me to stay with yet another Christian family, hence their benevolent nature. They were my biggest cheerleaders., and were very encouraging. My first order of business was to be gainfully employed. In very little time, I landed a job as a dishwasher at Shoney's Restaurant a few blocks away. Shoney's was a family style place with an Inn attached and it's close proximity to our house was convenient because I still didn't have a car.

Working the dish pit during breakfast and lunch was an interesting endeavor. It was kind of like attempting to run upward on a very fast downward moving escalator, in a steam room, while wearing a heavy sweat suit and work boots. The onslaught of dirty dishes was never-ending. Talk about constantly being in the weeds! As with the escalator, if you stopped to take a breather you quickly found yourself back at the bottom again.

During volume (busy times) there were two of us, one running the dish machine and one on the three-bay sinks. The three-bay was where all of the pots were scrubbed using good old-fashioned elbow grease. There were three sinks because the Health Department had very specific codes. The first sink was filled with soapy water for washing, the second was clean water for rinsing, and the third was for sanitizing. It was filled with water combined with a sanitizer solution from a unit on the wall, that was then dispensed down through a tube into the sink water. The Health Department also stipulated that no dishes or pots could be hand-dried with a towel; everything must air-dry. The guy on the three-bays would also serve as the clean plate runner. This meant that as the clean plates, bowls, and saucers were stacked on the metal counter after exiting the dish machine, it was his job to run them back up to the cooks' line so the circle of life could continue.

This was where I can probably say *"it"* happened for me. With arms loaded with stacks of clean plates, I would nimbly make my way down the line past the gas burner stoves, the searing hot flat top griddle, the hulking metal ovens, and the crackling hot fryers. I felt the change in climate immediately. My steamy escalator was like the balmy Florida Keys compared to this fiery hell of a location. Even my black denim jeans and heavy polo shirt gave way to these intense temperatures. My skinny arms attested to the severe weather change, as they felt the piercing heat from the stove burners while scampering by and delivering my wares. The line cooks worked at a frenzied pace, with movements that were swift, yet calculated. Turning, stepping, bending, reaching. It seemed hectic, yet efficient. It was organized chaos, and I loved it!

Instantly I was hooked. The cooks were warriors doing battle against that venerable ticket wheel. It sat in the pick-up window swiveling on its pedestal, as waiters and waitresses clipped tickets to it and the lead cook spun it around, dislodged each ticket, and clipped them on his ticket rail in line behind the other hundred tickets. He would then bark out the orders to the other line cooks. Our lead cook's name was Mark, and he wore his hat turned at a 45 degree angle to one side. I presume it was less about style, and more born out of function to allow better vision around the bill of his hat when looking up trying to read the tickets. He was roughly in his mid to late thirties with salt and pepper hair and a gold tooth. I nicknamed him Al Green because I thought he looked like the R&B singer turned Gospel singer. He was the fearless leader, and I wanted to learn from him.

Before I could earn that chance, I had to do a tour of duty through the prep department first. This position was a bridge between dish dog and line warrior. I say this because as prep cooks, we worked in the large prep kitchen behind the cook's line (also called the hot line or simply the line). We were adjacent to the dish area. If the dish crew started to go down, the prep cooks had to jump in and help out. I was quickly learning we were a team. There was no room for an "every man for himself" mentality. This was a principle that existed in every venue I worked in from henceforth.

It was the prep cooks' job to prepare all of the soups and sauces, cut vegetables, pre-cook and portion pasta, wash and cut salad greens, peel and cut potatoes, chop tomatoes, etc. Basically, all of the menial and tedious tasks that the line cooks would never have the time nor the space to do on the line. It is affectionately sometimes referred to as KP duty (short for Kitchen Prep duty). It can either be a blessing or a curse, depending on the disposition of the person. It is a job built on routine, to the point of monotony, for someone with attention issues like me. But it is a necessary evil in the average full service restaurant.

Shoney's served breakfast, lunch, and dinner, so we had to be to work at 5:00am every morning in order to get everything prepped for the entire day. This position is where a cook learns basic knife skills and efficiency. You also learn to clean up after yourself and to keep your work station organized. It is an introduction to multi-tasking, which will be *burned* into you should you make it to line cook status. We would begin every morning by turning on all of the equipment (ovens, steamer, large tilt skillet, steam kettle, etc.). The kitchen manager wrote out the prep list while taking inventory of what items were needed and the quantity. There were two of us, and we both had a specific list from which to work. It was, at times, the bane of my existence. I'm a person that needs to be able to quickly complete a task, and move on to the next one. I also like when each day is different from the previous. Unfortunately, the prep department works best when there are as few surprises as possible...every day is the same.

There were, however, two days of the week that did differ from the rest. These were referred to as "truck day." In my opinion, these were the worst two days each week. We would get a huge delivery to restock everything from freezer items, to cooler items, to dry goods. I hated those days because it was the prep cooks' job to put all of that stuff away, and still get all of our regular duties completed. I did, however, learn a few other very important lessons in this position.

The first, was how to follow a recipe. It sounds simple, but it goes far beyond cooking. I am generally a creative person. As a young and energetic individual, I was eager to "do my thing" in the kitchen. I learned how to slow down and simulate someone else's great ideas first. There are reasons why recipes have things done a certain way, and in a particular order. I usually found that out when I tried to use my own technique, skip a step, or do it out of sequence. Gleaning valuable skills, I was able to in time create my own great ideas (granted that part took years and I'm still perfecting my culinary ideas).

God would build on this lesson throughout the rest of my career, and in my personal life. It harkens back to "respecting the process." God has certain recipes for our success in all areas of life and I have seen personally what happens when I follow His recipe, and what happens when I don't. Of course...I'm still a work in progress!

A second lesson was that I realized the importance of the order of operations, if you will. This is similar to the recipe lesson but on a broader scale. In mathematics, the order of operations is known as BPMDAS (But Please Excuse My Dear Aunt Susie). A pneumonic device for remembering how to solve an algebra problem: brackets, parentheses, multiplication, division, addition then subtraction. I quickly observed the divine order upon which a properly functioning full-service kitchen works. This was fortified as I finally journeyed to fill my slot on the cooks' line. I was now able to understand the path of a simple tomato, for instance. From delivery through the back door, to proper storage, to skillfully processing, placing in a labeled container, then rotating behind older product, and finally sauteing it into an omelet, and sending out to the customer to enjoy. With that, I was absorbing how each department in the kitchen relied on each other in order to function as a well-oiled machine.

Upon my advance to the line, Mr. Al Green (A.K.A. Mark) started with teaching me the importance of properly stocking my station. In other words, if you fail to plan, then you plan to fail. This lesson was no joke! I would come face-to-face with this same concept in a brutal way during a job much later in my career. Now God was building on the previous lesson of doing my best and standing by my work. I quickly found that being properly prepared would allow my best to be at a higher level. In other words, if an engine is firing on all cylinders, then its maximized potential is a lot higher than an engine firing on only half of it's cylinders. No matter how hard you drive the engine, it only has so much potential due to pre-determined limitations. Mark, along with that mighty ticket wheel, taught me to always prepare my station ahead of time.

Another lesson I learned on the line was how to be lightning fast, yet deadly accurate. Though breakfast cooks don't get many accolades in the world of restaurant cookery, they have my utmost respect. During breakfast service, the ticket times are much faster than lunch or dinner. This simply means you have less time that the servers, and ultimately the customers, expect to wait for food. You will easily find yourself with four saute pans going at one time, with two eggs in each. One pan may be over easy, the other sunny-side up, and the other two may be over-medium. You have to crack and cook the sunny-side ups without breaking the yolks, while making sure the white is done, and then get them on the plate without breaking those yolks. The over-easies and over-mediums must be flipped without breaking the yolks, while being careful not to overcook them. Over-easy can quickly travel from easy to medium and mediums can become well in the blink of an eye. All of this while toasting the proper type of bread (wheat, white or rye) and working hash browns. Let's not forget about dispensing three perfect disks of batter onto the flat top griddle for a side of pancakes, while being careful to flip them without ripping or burning them. This may all be on one ticket. Just five more tickets hanging!

There was typically one cook for the first couple of hours during breakfast, so once that ticket wheel started spinning, you better have been locked and loaded. We had a hotel as part of the same property, so when the census was high at the Inn, we would really be in for a rough ride. As everyone knows, breakfast is a must for most people staying in a hotel.

We would have "change-over" from breakfast to lunch at about 11:00am. This was a perfect example of that organized chaos

I mentioned earlier. The two cooks would have the remaining breakfast orders working, while also cooking lunch food. The servers would also be going through changes in the dining room like changing of menus, specials of the day, etc. We had to phase into lunch while breaking down all of the product from breakfast, wrap it, and put it in the walk-in cooler in the prep kitchen. Attention to detail was key, because it could be very easy to miss an item on a ticket, or an entire ticket, while performing a hundred different tasks during this time.

Besides proper egg preparation, I would say the other major culinary skill I learned while working the line was how to cook meats to the right temperature. We served a lot of burgers at Shoney's, which had a menu comparable to a Denny's. Unlike IHOP, we didn't serve breakfast all day (PRAISE GOD!). We also sold steaks during dinner service. Cooking a piece of meat to rare, medium-rare, medium, medium-well, or well, is referred to as it's temperature because there is a specific internal temperature that corresponds with each level of doneness. I learned how to judge the doneness of a burger based on length of time on the griddle, color of the meat, and the feel when lightly pressed with the spatula.

Probably the greatest food concept I learned, was something called *carry-over cooking*. This is the principle that food continues to cook after being taken out of its cooking environment. In practical terms, this means a piece of fried fish continues to cook after it has been removed from the fryer. Rice continues to cook after the pot has been removed from the burner. *All* food experiences carry-over cooking (vegetables, meats, fish, pasta, grains, etc.). I experienced this concept in full swing, as I over-cooked quite a few orders of over-easy eggs and medium-rare burgers. With the help of Al Green yelling at me, and the servers impatiently huffing and puffing, I had a shortened learning curve. I quickly "got busy on the wheels of steel", as I liked to say. My trial by fire being complete (for the time-being), I eventually secured a spot as a starting line cook on dinner shift.

Spiritually, this was a pretty interesting time for me because I was rapidly becoming more urbanized. I began riding with my friend on his Honda Ninja motorcycle to a night club called Rumors. We wouldn't even go inside. At about 1am, when the club was near closing, there would gather a huge crowd and we would just stand next to the bike and girl watch. As a nineteen year-old from the burbs, this was intoxicating to me, and I was becoming addicted to the "night life."

On Sundays, everybody would gather at Copleland Park on 15th street in an area of Tampa nick-named "suitcase city." This was due to all the transience of people moving in and out of the many apartment complexes that dotted the area. We used to ride the Ninja to the park and again, chill while girl watching. I was getting sucked further and further into the urban culture. Interestingly enough, the more urbanized I became, the less criminal I became. I did, however, go on to make some insanely bad decisions.

Part of the problem was my drinking, which actually was illegal because I was only 19 years old. Being that I was now working at night, my waking hours had changed. There is also a strong subculture in the hospitality industry, in which everyone enjoys "drinks after work." I started sleeping later into the day and working (and partying) later into the night. I had jumped head-long into carnality and wasn't feeding my spirit man at all.

As humans, we are made in God's likeness, in that we are a trinity just as He is. We have a spirit that lives in a body which has a soul. Our spirit is in communication with God's Spirit, while our fleshly body is in communication with the physical world around us. The soul is the mediator between the two. Our soul is where the mind, will and emotions reside. It is our central processing center, if you will.

All of the data from the spirit realm and the physical realm are collected and processed in the soul. The problem is that often it receives conflicting information. Our mind perceives certain notions, like philosophy and intellect, while our will gives unction to move. The emotions provide inner feeling which fuels the mind and the will. This three-part processing center is the battleground. Whatever controls the soul is what reigns over the entire person. Like all things under God's design, whatever we feed, is what will grow stronger. Well, I was feeding the flesh, and not the spirit, so the voice of my physical struggles was much stronger. My soul was getting overwhelmed with physical input and responding accordingly. I wasn't giving my soul any spiritual input.

In Romans 12:2 Paul tells us, "Do not conform to this world, but be transformed with the renewing of your mind." I wasn't renewing my mind. Carnal data was bombarding my soul and therefore I was responding accordingly. My emotions were ruling the day, and I made erratic decisions all the time. One day I'm here, the next day I'm there. Which is exactly what happened eventually. I left the supportive environment of this loving Christian family and found myself sharing an apartment in the middle of suitcase city with a drug dealer.

I decided to quit my job at Shoney's due to frustrations with the management. So, I took a summer job working in the Parking Services Division at USF (The University of South Florida) which is located just west of Thonotosassa, in an area of Tampa called Temple Terrace. It's about midway between Thonotosassa and suitcase city. While working at USF, I met a guy who was friends with a girl I had started dating. After that summer job ended, I got a job working with him as a door-to-door Tampa Tribune salesman.

Soon, I broke-up with that girl, and was no longer living with the family in Thonotosassa. Needing a place to stay, my fellow newspaper salesman let me move in with him. It turned out that he was just eighteen years old and was already on probation for a drug charge. He had to have gainful employment as part of his probation. The apartment had one bedroom with one bathroom so I crashed on the recliner in the living room every night. I remember we were so poor, we couldn't afford a place with central air and heat. The heater was a window unit in the bedroom. When winter approached he slept with his bedroom door closed to keep the heat in. Naturally, it made the temperature drop in the front where I was sleeping. I had to sleep with the oven open and turned on all night.

A neighbor gave us an old iron so we could iron our clothes every day. This thing was so old it was just a metal hot plate with a handle and an electrical cord attached to it. When you plugged it in, it would heat up and just keep getting hotter because there was no temperature control. We would have to plug it in, let it heat up, unplug it, wrap a towel around the handle (so we could hold it without burning ourselves), and then iron our clothes. One day, I came home and my roommate was gone. As soon as I came in the door, I noticed the iron sitting on the kitchen counter. He had left it plugged in and the metal was actually glowing red! I immediately hurried over and unplugged it. Even the plug was hot. Thanks be to God that thing didn't start to melt the counter.

Eventually, he got tired of not making enough money to cover the bills, and he started selling drugs again. He approached me about "putting me on" (hooking me up with his supplier so I could start selling). My response was, "Well you know how I feel about that." He replied, "And you know how I feel about being homeless!" I had been homeless before and the prospect of that didn't scare me nearly as much as the thought of doing hard time for a drug charge.

If there was ever a time that the All Mighty Hand of God was on my life, this was definitely that season. Though I resisted the temptation to sell drugs, I did go on to make some horrendous decisions. We used to ride around with his friend who had a Chevy Bronco, who was actually one of his customers. I think he gave him a price break, in exchange for transportation. We also used to ride with another one of his friends, who wasn't a narcotics dealer nor a user. He was however, an avid weed head, which pretty much everyone we hung out with was. He was an aspiring rapper who practiced when he wasn't working. He and I used to have friendly rap duels just to sharpen our skills. I was, and still am, into writing poetry, so rapping came naturally. As a matter of fact, years earlier I would to take my little sister for walks through our neighborhood and freestyle to amuse her.

My roommate started out by going to a drug house and selling. I rode with him because he said he wanted someone to watch his back. That was laughable, as I was too busy drinking to be of any use. Soon he bought a car, and we used to ride around on 15th Street between Fowler Avenue and Fletcher Avenue as he scouted out his territory. It was only a very short distance, but there was a huge problem with it. He had no tags and no license. I was riding shotgun all the way. How moronic can you get?! Soon, we started riding with his dad to the projects, and hanging out with his dad's girlfriend and her family. This was someone else's territory, so I don't really recall my roommate selling whenever we were there. There was another twist to the plot. His dad's girlfriend was hooked on crack cocaine.

This was a habit that his dad objected to; I believe he was actually trying to help her quit. At one point, her sister was in town from New York. One day I was hanging out in the projects with him. As we were getting ready to leave, he somehow caught his girl taking a hit of crack. He brought her out into the front yard and started to beat her. I was in the passenger side of the car with my hand on the door handle, ready to jump out and grab him. God has always caused me to be observant, which stems from my dad drilling it into my brother and I when we were growing up. He would always say, "Pay attention to your surrounds." Well, right at that moment, I happened to look over to the left and saw her sister standing in the doorway of the house. Then she turned without saying anything and went back inside. Now, I knew she was kind of hot-headed. I instinctually jumped out of the car and headed straight for the doorway of the house. Just as I reached the front step...BOOM! I ran right into her as she was carrying a knife she had gotten from the kitchen. I blocked the doorway and talked her off the ledge so to speak. I knew she would listen to me because she and I were very cool with each other. I told her we would leave immediately, but she needed to chill out. Once I got her to put down the knife, I grabbed my roommate's dad and we got out of dodge!

I don't remember going back to the projects after that. I did, however, start hanging out with a friend of my roommate named Robert and his crew. Once again they were druggies. They were doing acid while smoking marijuana. God truly kept his hand on me, because although I smoked weed with them, I never dropped acid. Any drug harder than marijuana just didn't interest me. As a matter of fact, I wasn't even really interested in marijuana. I mostly did it because everyone I was hanging with was smoking it. There couldn't be any more of a textbook case of giving in to peer pressure than that. I thank God for his abundant grace and mercy. I was truly that prodigal child that had strayed far, far away from my Father's house. What's so incredibly humbling is that, though I had run far away from Him, he stuck right by me all of that time. There is no God like the Living God.

There was one day in particular that seemed like it was taken from the script of a movie. Robert and I had decided we wanted to go to a night club called Uptown 21. Neither one of us had ever been before, but for some odd reason, I just really wanted to go on this particular night. The only problem was, we had no vehicle. This club was for people 21 years and older. On Sunday nights though, it was 18 and up. Well it was Sunday and we were itching to go. Rob had tried to convince one of the guys in the crew to give us a ride. He said he would, but there was just one ginormous problem. When Rob spoke to him on the phone, he said his car had been stolen earlier that day. What was strange was that he said he was sure he knew who had stolen it. Rob and I caught the bus out to this guy's house in West Tampa, and we started trying to put the pieces of the puzzle together. The guy had somehow gotten word that a teenage girl they knew had apparently run away from home the day before and stolen his car.

To this day, I have no clue how he came by that information but he was absolutely convinced that this runaway girl had his car. Now we had a lead, but there was just one more snag. We had no vehicle to track her down in. They mentioned another guy they knew, but really didn't want to use him as an option. They were like, "We could ask Bolivia." I said, "Bolivia?!" They said, "Yeah, everybody just calls him that because he's from Bolivia but we don't know his real name." I was thinking, "Well, what's wrong with using him for a ride?" They said, "It's hard to talk to him because he doesn't speak good English. Also, he can't see, so you have to tell him where to turn while he's driving." Alarm bells went off in my head. I was thinking, "Whaaaat?!!! How did he even *get* a license?!"

As we thought about it for a while, desperation was starting to set in. Desperate times call for desperate measures. We decided to brave it. This guy Bolivia was our only hope. We walked over to his house and the guy he lived with helped us translate. He agreed to help us out. Boy was this going to be a bumpy ride. I sat in the back along with Rob. The guy whose car got stolen sat in the front passenger's seat, so he could direct Bolivia. After a trip filled with various hand gestures and super broken English, they actually got us to the neighborhood where this girl's parents lived. We drove around for a few minutes in the vicinity to see if we could spot his car. He then pointed Bolivia in the direction of her parent's house. The plan was to speak to her parents to find out any vital information.

As we drove toward the house, *his* car suddenly came speeding by us heading in the opposite direction. As the car passed, they recognized not only the girl driving, but also the girl in the passenger side. He was right; this teenage girl actually had stolen his car. He was also correct in thinking she may be hanging out in the area around her parent's house. Who knew?! Rob and the guy yelled for them to stop. Bolivia pulled into a nearby driveway to turn the car around. Rob and the guy both jumped out and started running after the two girls, who decided to ditch the stolen car. Meanwhile, I found myself in the middle of the back seat of this old clunker sweating bullets. My man Bolivia was frantically fighting with the shift-on-the-column to put it in reverse and back out of the driveway. At this point, I was trying every hand gesture and unction I could think of to get him to just pull the car over. Thankfully, he ended up stopping and I got out and waited for the other two to return. The ordeal was finally over.

Later that night we actually did make it to Uptown 21. After a while, Rob and the other guy wanted to go to another club, but I wanted to stay. They decided to leave and said they would come back and get me later. The guy was over 21, so he gave me his wrist band before he left so I could order something to drink. It was on now. I sat at the bar and ordered a pitcher of beer. I was drinking, minding my own business and enjoying the music. After a while, somebody came by and hit me on the shoulder. When I looked up to see who it was, I saw this lady just looking at me. It took me a moment to focus. I was thinking, "Why is this lady standing there looking at me?" Then I realized it was Lisa! After an awkward moment, I came to myself and was like, "Hey, how are you?!" We chatted for a while, then we hit the dance floor. As we were dancing, she was suddenly snatched away from me. It was her ex-boyfriend. Only, he didn't realize he was her ex-boyfriend. He thought he was her *current* boyfriend.

Again, God is good all the time. Even though I seemed to have a bad temper any other time, when I was drinking, I was more relaxed. I just looked at the two of them arguing on the dance floor and I walked back to the bar, sat down and continued drinking my beer. I figured that was an A-B conversation and I was going to C my way out of it.

I never caught back up with her that night, but I did end up calling her house and speaking to her mom a couple of days later. Her mom gave her the message, and we finally met up for a casual date. When I told her about the crazy stuff that happened before we had run into each other that night in the club, she told me that she had an equally interesting experience that day en-route to the club. We chalked it up to fate and had a good laugh. We soon were dating again, and I started going to church with her. I even joined the youth choir (which was actually older youth and young adults) with her and her friends.

Sometime later, my roommate and I got into a big argument and he asked me to move out. In Proverbs 22:6 it says, "Train up a child in the way he should go and when he is older he will not depart from it." You can take the child away from the military upbringing, but you can't take the military upbringing out of the child. The values that were instilled in me while growing up were keeping me from seeing eye-to-eye with my roommate. He had a certain way of dealing with things that was not my way, and it eventually led to us having to part ways. God was saving me...no, he was literally saving me.

I was in desperate need of a new place to live. I soon moved into another apartment on the front side of our complex. One day, I was hanging out with my neighbors in front of our apartments, when we saw "Green Team" roll into the complex. Green Team was the nickname for the Hillsborough County Sheriff Deputies, because their colors are green and white. They were riding in the two undercover vehicles we always saw them driving through the hood. They were actually confiscated from some earlier bust. We watched as they drove up to my old apartment, got out a battering ram, broke down the front door, and raided the apartment. Thanks be to God for a disagreement between roommates, which had temporarily left me in need of a place to stay. Like I said, I'd rather be homeless than do hard time on drug charges. Even though I hadn't been selling I had definitely been in the wrong place on too many occasions during that season, and it could have ended up being at the wrong time. Again, God had saved me.

While all of this was happening, I quit the Tribune job and started working at Miami Subs, and then Fuddrucker's. This was a build-your-own-burger type of joint, which served quarter pound and half pound patties. Here, I further improved my skills with cooking meat to a specific temperature. I had conquered the "turn and burn" and was enjoying the culinary ride. However, there was trouble on the horizon. That last episode of watching the police kick-in my old roommate's front door helped push me back into reading and studying God's Word. Unfortunately, as we well know, the moment we commit to serving God, we can be sure the enemy is soon to show up. About a year into the job, I left Fuddruckers because I got into a heated disagreement with the assistant manager. Thanks to my bad temper, I was only able to take so much and eventually exploded one day. It seemed to me like this manager was singling me out on a regular basis. He may have been or he may not have been. Either way, my actions were very unbecoming of someone who claimed to know Christ. The issue is that I fell right into the trap the enemy had set. Justified or unjustified, offense is always a trap just waiting to take you down. It causes us to do things that ruin our testimony in front of non-believers. After using some choice words, I walked out and was once again in search of a job.

"Mid-way through a meal involving spicy tomato sauce, one may consume some wine to ease the burst of flavor before continuing the dish."

~NME

Chapter 3:

INTERMEZZO

~SORBETO *ALL' ARRABIATA*~

T he third chapter of my culinary career can be characterized as the Intermezzo (*inter-metso*). This term has a similar meaning over a variety of art forms. According to Merriam-Webster, in music, it is a movement placed between the major sections of an extended piece of music. In the culinary world, it is a very small, intermediate serving within a multi-course menu. It typically serves as a palate cleanser as the menu changes directions. Many times it's a single, small scoop of sorbet commonly made of raspberry, mint or even parsley. It's so small that a special utensil is used to serve it, called aptly enough…a sorbet scoop. Most often it precedes a shift toward the heavier courses.

I decided to call this portion of my professional life the Intermezzo because I took a brief sojourn away from cooking, and into the supermarket and call center worlds. You could say it was a brief movement between the major sections of this extended piece of music. The term arrabiata is an Italian word meaning angry. It is used to describe a spicy tomato sauce containing tomatoes, olive oil, garlic and red pepper flakes. Sorbeto all' Arrabiata would literally mean sorbet served "angry-style." I can honestly say these two jobs just about drove me nuts! As you read this chapter, it's title will make perfect sense.

It wasn't long after walking out of Fuddrucker's that I secured a bag boy job at the U Save Grocery Store on Fletcher Avenue and 30th Street (I think it's an Aldi Grocery now). This job was further away and I still didn't own a car. It was now summer, and our classic Florida late afternoon showers were in full swing. My shift just so happened to start at about 4 or 5pm, so I prayed before beginning my walk to work each day. Sure enough, like clockwork, the rain would hold off until I got there and then the heavens would let loose! It sounds simple and corny, but the Lord was teaching me to trust in Him daily. I had worked in a grocery store before, so the job wasn't a totally foreign experience. This is by the way, exactly how the intermezzo course of a meal works. It draws on some flavor from the earlier, lighter part of the meal and ties it into the upcoming courses.

Only a few months after starting that job, it once again seemed to me like a particular manager was always hounding me. This time it was one of the assistant managers and I thought she just didn't like men. I have since found that when I continue to encounter the same issue over and over, it is most likely something working in me. Seeing as how I hadn't learned that lesson yet, there came a day when I had had enough. While on my evening break, I went to the break room, grabbed my back pack, clocked out, and walked out the front door never to return.

As usual God provided yet again. This time, I quickly got offered a job at the Burger King in the same shopping center as the U Save. I didn't take that position though, because my girlfriend and I had gotten an apartment some distance away. I was able to get a job at the call center where she worked instead. This was a job at which I had no chance of succeeding. We all had our own little cubicle space with a computer, a headset, and a mic. We were doing collections for a magazine company of all things. I quickly realized that I was absolutely not about to heckle someone over a balance owed on a magazine subscription that was sent to collections. Another problem for me was having to sit in a confined space all evening. Talk about ants in your pants! I used to have to get up about every half hour and walk around the office.

We had this one hot shot collector on the team who was about thirty-one years old and he used to get on my last nerve. Back then I had an issue with just about everybody. He used to always try to hit on some of the ladies in the office. One day, he made my girlfriend upset for some reason that I can't even remember now. Yet again, I went off like a bomb. I approached him in the break room, got in his face, and started yelling and cursing at him. I was 5'10" and only weighed about 180 pounds and was threatening to do him some bodily harm. Thanks be to God he didn't take me up on the offer to "settle it like men." Needless to say the head manager called me into his office and had a conference with me. It ended of course, with my termination. It was glaringly obvious to the average onlooker, but I didn't even think I had an issue with my temper. I honestly didn't.

Well, I had blown another job that the Lord had gifted to me. We had just moved into our new place on September 23, 1994 and I was already out of work by about November. I needed to find another job and fast. Though I enjoyed not coming home sweaty and smelling like food every night, I missed the action. The kitchen was calling me to return to the line of work that I felt I was better suited for. This hiatus from the kitchen did serve as a refreshment of sorts though. It had been a brief break from the preliminary parts of the menu. In addition, it was a palate cleanser in preparation for the heavier courses that were about to follow. I am reminded of a line in the movie *Return of the King* (the second of *The Lord of the Rings* trilogy). There is a scene in which Pippin the hobbit and Gandalf the white wizard await the start of an impending battle. Speaking with a voice trembling with fear, Pippin says to Gandalf, "It's so quiet." Gandalf simply replies, "It's the deep breath before the plunge." I didn't know it at the time, but through this very brief season I was actually being prepared for the "deep plunge" that I was about to experience personally, professionally, and spiritually.

"One must not stress over what meats to accompany their greens, as much as if the meats themselves compliment each other for harmonic flavors."

~NME

Chapter 4:
~ ITALIAN WEDDING SOUP ~

"The term "wedding soup" is a mistranslation of the Italian language phrase "minestra maritata ("married soup"),” which is a reference to the fact that green vegetables and meats go well together. Some form of minestra maritata was long popular in Toledo, Spain, before pasta became an affordable commodity to most Spaniards. The modern wedding soup is quite a bit lighter than the old Spanish form, which contained more meats than just the meatballs of modern Italian-American versions.”

Diana Nelson Jones, Food Historian

Lisa and I had moved into our new apartment in September. and by November, I was in search of another job. Our apartment complex was on the corner of Himes Avenue and Waters Avenue in an area of Tampa called Carrollwood. It was a nice one bedroom, one bathroom place on the second floor. My mom had given us a sofa and love seat until we were able to buy some new furniture.

Prior to getting fired from that Tele-collections job, there was one Sunday that still stands out very prominently to me. I had been pondering something for a while, and finally reached a resolve the previous night. That next morning was Sunday, and we didn't attend church for some reason. Instead, Lisa and her mom went out shopping. They were gone forever, and I was growing impatient because we still had to go to work that evening at the call center. Eventually, they got home in just enough time for us to head off to work. But I had a surprise first. After her mom left, I said a few words to Lisa. Then, I timidly got down on one knee, and popped The Question. I had it all mapped out. I would propose on that Sunday. We would get married on the first day of the New Year, which I knew was also going to be a Sunday. But wait…first she had to say yes. As I said the words, "Will you marry me?" she giggled and immediately said yes. We both went to work that evening, probably beaming.

Now fast forward about a month, and the joblessness issue takes on a whole new light. We had decided I would work as much as I could and she would stay home and do all of the planning and coordinating. We figured not having to pay a wedding planner would make up for her lost income. Upon leaving that job, she used her final paycheck to buy her gown from David's Bridal.

I found a job working as a prep cook at a privately owned Italian steakhouse called Iavarone's (pronounced I-varone-es). It was in walking distance, which helped because we only had one car. I walked to work every morning and she was able to use the car for running errands. Iavarone's was, and still is, after all of these years a favorite among the locals. It was my first steakhouse experience, and my first job cooking Italian cuisine. I jumped right in and began learning everything I could.

The first concept I remember learning was something called *standard breading procedure*. This was the process we used to prep the onion rings. It's a classic three-step technique used for preparing foods to be fried. We actually made it a four-step process by adding a step to the beginning. We would start by dipping the product into milk wash which is simply a milk bath. This step was vital because it moistened the surface of the onions so the breading would adhere. Step two was to drain off the excess liquid and place the rings into flour. Being fully coated, they were gently shaken to remove the excess flour and placed into an egg wash. This is just raw eggs beaten together with a splash of water added. It was important to make sure all the floured surface of each ring was coated with egg otherwise the breading would fall off. The final step in this process was to drain off the excess egg and place them into bread crumbs. They had to be firmly pressed into the crumbs so as to allow for a uniformly breaded finish. They were then placed on sheet trays lined with parchment paper and stored in the walk-in freezer.

I found out that the *standard breading procedure* could be used for coating a wide variety of items in preparation for deep frying or pan frying. In fact, we also used this technique for preparing our chicken parmesan. Quickly, I also realized that this was the exact process by which we prepared the extra crispy chicken back at KFC (minus the added milk wash of course). They say practice makes perfect and I can honestly say, I got plenty of practice. The monotony was back, just like at Shoney's, but I hung in there. Again, the point was driven home about working quickly and neatly.

I learned that the key to successfully navigating this standard breading procedure, without winding up with plaster all over your hands, was keeping a "wet hand/dry hand" approach. It's called that because you literally keep one hand wet and the other hand dry. Use one hand to take the rings out of the milk wash and subsequent egg wash. Use the other hand to dredge them in the flour and the bread crumbs. There were a few days when I ended up with two heavy catcher's mitts for hands, due to all of the milk-flour-egg-bread crumb plaster. Without the "wet hand/dry hand" technique, you basically use the standard breading procedure to bread your own fingers. That's fine I guess, as long as you don't plan on deep frying them when you're finished!

Another preparation I learned was Caesar dressing. I don't remember that exact recipe, but it actually doesn't really matter. Part of the beauty of cooking is that when you learn the basics, you are then able to create and recreate with accuracy and proficiency. In other words, once the concepts are instilled in you, you can use what's on the inside to fuel continual new culinary creations.

The basic concept with Caesar dressing is about creating an emulsion using raw eggs, vinegar, and oil. An emulsion is the combining of two substances that otherwise don't combine. Oil and vinegar are a great example. They actually *can* be combined you just need to give them an *emulsifying ingredient,* along with some air. Eggs are an emulsifier and so is mustard. Caesar dressing contains lots of eggs and a little Dijon mustard, which help bring everybody together. It also contains vinegar, lemon juice, Worcestershire sauce, garlic, oil, parmesan cheese, salt, pepper, and yes…even anchovies! Naturally, the oil won't combine with the vinegar, lemon juice, and Worcestershire sauce. This is where the power of the eggs and mustard come into play (besides adding flavor). It is also where that lesson about doing things in the right order came back into play. I learned that the mixture won't emulsify correctly if everything is just thrown in together all at once. This will cause it to separate or "break." The oil is *not* an initial member of the team. The mixture must be vigorously blended together using a hand-held emersion blender or a standard table top blender, depending on the batch size. Once everything is blended, the oil is now slowly streamed into the blended mixture while the blender is still running. The circular motion causes air to be whipped into it. The fat molecules (the oil) and the liquid molecules become suspended between the air molecules. They are all now one homogenous unit. As before at Shoney's, I saw first-hand what happens when you try to do things out of sequence. I had a couple of batches of Caesar dressing that ended up looking more like a hot mess. Fortunately for me, the Chef showed me how to fix a broken Caesar dressing. Thank God for the plan of restoration. The only way to successfully fix it though, was to again follow a specific procedure. So either way, patience was going to lead to a perfect product.

Caesar dressing is just an altered version of a style of dressing known as a *vinaigrette*, which would have a different ratio of similar ingredients. A vinaigrette consists of three parts fat (usually an oil) and one part acid (usually some kind of vinegar). Add whatever other flavor you want, and stir. It's that simple. The mixture will however, naturally separate after a few moments. If you prefer a creamier vinaigrette, you can add an egg yolk or a little mustard and vigorously whisk it. It can also be put into a jar with a lid and shaken. The resulting emulsion will be lighter in color and have a creamy consistency.

Now the possibilities are endless. Some other form of fat can be substituted for the oil, and a different acid can be substituted for the vinegar. Warm bacon vinaigrette, a classic dressing for spinach salad, is a perfect example. Melted bacon fat is used in place of the oil, with red wine vinegar and bacon bits for flavorings. Citrus vinaigrettes are common on salads here in Florida. They simply incorporate a citrus juice in place of vinegar for the acid component. This does sometimes require the juice to be "reduced", which simply means cooking it down so the flavor is intensified, and it has a thicker consistency. I also learned that there are ways to address certain special situations. For instance, some people get nervous about using raw eggs in a product that isn't going to be cooked. A great substitute is mayonnaise. Mayo is in fact an emulsion itself. It's just eggs, oil, lemon (or mustard), salt and pepper. The difference is that if you use store-bought mayo, it has been processed so as not to cause any food borne illness from the eggs. This will work in both your Caesar dressing *and* your vinaigrette.

For a short time, I also took on a night job at Hopp's Bar and Grill. It was a micro-brewery concept that served a few of their own beers, as well as offering commercially produced standards. Back then in 1994, Hopp's was the only micro-brewery game in town. Nowadays, Tampa has become a well-known brewing town. Upon starting there, my culinary skills weren't proven yet, so I had to start back in the dish pit. It was insanely busy! After about a week, I got a shot as a line cook and my performance wasn't up to scratch, so I took a second tour in the dish pit. Soon after, I got another shot on the line, and I didn't blow it this time. I really started sharpening my skills between both jobs. Every day I walked to Iavarone's at 9am and worked until about 2pm. Then I went home to rest for about an hour, and then drove to Hopp's and worked until 1am on week nights and 2am on Friday and Saturday nights. This was what Lisa and I used to call "working with a hump in your back." I drove myself to work because I didn't want Lisa having to get up and drive to get me at that hour every night. I remember being so tired that there were times when I would be driving home at 3am in a complete daze. About half way into the trip, I would suddenly become conscious of where I was. It would scare me because I didn't even know if I had run any red lights.

Thankfully, I got promoted to line cook for the dinner shift at Iavarone's and left the Hopp's position. But there was a wedding to pay for, so I still needed to work as much as possible. I began doing double shifts. Prep cook by day and line cook by night. It was pretty cool actually, because I was really learning a tremendous amount about all things food. I remember learning about *blanching* and *shocking*. We sold a ton of pasta, so we used to par-cook or blanch batches of each type and store them in the walk-in refrigerator. When blanching pasta you want to cook it until it is *al dente,* which is an Italian term literally meaning "to the tooth." It quickly became apparent to me that over-crowding the pot is a very bad idea. I wound up with a pot full of pasta "knuckles" a few times. Yet again, that old lesson of taking the time to do things the proper way and not being hasty.

Once the pasta is cooked al dente, it must be very quickly cooled or *shocked* in ice water. This is due to that concept we discussed earlier called *carry-over cooking.* You want to stop the cooking process as abruptly as possible so as not to allow the pasta to over-cook. I went on to use the technique of *blanching and shocking* at every cooking job I would ever have from that time forward. It is a staple principal in restaurant cooking.

In no time at all the big day had arrived. It was Sunday January 1, 1995. TIME FOR A WEDDING! All of my hard work in the kitchen and all of Lisa's hard work planning and coordinating had led to this moment. We made it. We had been able to completely plan and pay for the entire wedding. Lisa and her mom had done a tremendous amount of work. Our colors were Royal Blue and White with Silver trim. It was one thing to run through the rehearsals a couple of times. But on that day when I stood at the Alter and watched as each couple in the court came down the aisle, it was an awesome site. The groom's men were wearing black tuxedos with royal blue cummerbunds. The bridesmaids were wearing elegant Royal blue dresses. It looked really nice. Lisa had done an awesome job envisioning what it would look like when it was all put together. I had on an all-white tux with a Royal blue handkerchief. Lisa's entrance was beautiful. She had on her white dress and her hair was in an up-doe. After the ceremony we enjoyed a nice reception at the clubhouse of a close friend. Then we made our escape. We had been gifted a one-night stay in a nice hotel on the Courtney Campbell Causeway. "The Causeway," as it is referred to, is on the intra-coastal waterway in the Tampa Bay. It is very scenic and relaxing. I took a week of unpaid vacation and we just enjoyed the moment.

All too quickly that week was over and the rigors of married life were about to begin. I returned to work and picked-up where I left off. Iavarone's is an Italian restaurant, but back then all of the kitchen staff was Hispanic except for the Sous Chef and the grill cook. Culinary French (which we will cover in the next chapter) is classically the official kitchen language. Here however, Spanish ruled the day and I thoroughly enjoyed it. It was one more thing for me to learn. I used to speak Spanish to them and they would speak English to me. This way we all were able to practice our foreign language skills.

Starting out on the line at the salad station, I worked with an ex-boxer from Puerto Rico. He was a tall drink of water that stood about 6' 4" and weighed about a buck-fifty. He was nothing but skin, bones, and muscle. He had about a 28-inch waist and had very broad shoulders. You could see every blood vessel running down his long arms with two weather-beaten anvils for fists. Though he was skinny, his arms were huge. He was probably in his late forties or early fifties then, and he was still very, very quick on his feet. I had to learn to move when he said move. I also had to navigate everything he would say to me. His extremely broken English was almost harder to understand than his mile-a-minute Spanish. It didn't take long for me to get in the groove of things, and he and I worked together very well. I went on to learn all of the stations, but sauté would be my home. The Executive chef took me under his wing and I became his evening shift assistant. In fact, I was very blessed because all of the guys took a liking to me. I was able to fit right in.

Unfortunately, I came to fit in a little too well. I began going and hanging out with the fellas after work. This may seem harmless but the problem was that I didn't know how to come home at a decent hour. My wife used to constantly be worried. We would usually hang out at one guy's house that lived in the apartment complex next to mine. I remember one occasion when Lisa actually found his apartment and knocked on the door to get me to come home. They were all single, so what they did was their business, but I should have known better. It hadn't been a year of marriage and I was already starting to resent it. I do believe that people can get married at a young age and have a successful marriage. I have come to realize though, that I wasn't ready at that age. I was too immature, and more importantly, I didn't know myself yet. What's worse is that I was completely unaware of the fact that I didn't know who I was.

Years later, I would serve under a Pastor that once said that there are three types of students: There are those who know that they know. There are those who know that they don't know. Then, there are those that don't know that they don't know. He said the third type of student is the hardest to lead. They not only do things incorrectly, but then don't want to be corrected so they can learn. I was that person; young and very head-strong in all of my ways. We would prove to have a very tough go of it.

"Change In food can allow for adaptation and interest in new flavors. Interest in new flavors can open opportunities for new styles of cooking."

~NME

Chapter 5:

~SQUAB WITH DUCHESS POTATOES, BITTER GREENS AND BEURRE ROUGE~

The seemingly odd title of this chapter will make much more sense later, as we work our way into the spiritual matters of my life during this season. Professionally, I came to refer to this period as "*My* culinary school." It's where my cooking traveled from "good home-style cooking" to "professional chef-style cooking." I call it "*My* culinary school", because it was basically just that. Conventional schooling hadn't been an option, so I had, until this point, learned from those around me. That included Mark from Shoney's, Chef Danny from Iavarone's, my father-in-law (a retired chef), and even my wife! Yes, she was my first culinary teacher (she had learned from her dad). Now I was about to learn an entirely new way of approaching food. It would become "*my* culinary school."

Around February of 1995, I started working at the Hyatt Regency Hotel in Downtown Tampa. I went back to the day shift at Iavarone's and worked the evening shift at the Hyatt. Shortly thereafter, I left Iavarone's altogether, and concentrated on my new job. It was definitely different from anything I was used to. The

Hyatt had a "wardrobe" department where I had to go every day to pick-up my uniform or "kitchen whites" as they are often called. This consisted of a white chef jacket, black and white hound's tooth pants, and a white neckerchief. My next stop was the locker room to change, and then down stairs to the kitchen. Once there, I retrieved the final part of my kitchen whites. That iconic hat known as the toque blanche.

The Hyatt kitchen was intimidatingly huge to me. It was my first time working in a multi-outlet operation. We had a Banquet department, Garde Manger, a restaurant called Pastabilities, and another restaurant called City Center Café. I was assigned to work in the City Center Café. The chef that was to be my direct supervisor was Darren Gidney. He was, in my opinion, the best teaching chef I would go on to work for throughout my entire culinary career.

I was twenty-one years old, and he was just a few years older than me, but he was an awesome teacher. He took me on as a pupil and really sought to develop me. His first order of business was to loan me a book that belonged to our executive chef. It was titled *Professional Cooking* by Wayne Gisslen. He would give me assignments and I had to go home and read about that subject in the book and have the answers when I returned to work. Though I ended up only working there for about five months, I learned more culinary lessons than I could discuss in this book. So, we shall cover a few that stand out.

Let's start with the uniform. The jacket and hat are traditionally white because it was originally thought to show cleanliness. The jacket is double breasted to allow it to be reversed if it gets stained during the shift. It also provides a double layer of protection against spillage of hot substances. The neckerchief was originally worn to absorb sweat while working long hours in the hot kitchen environment. The toque blanche (toke-blonk), or simply "toque", has many vertical pleats around it to symbolize the 100 different ways a chef can prepare an egg. We typically wear a paper version of the toque nowadays, so it can be discarded for a new one if it gets soiled while working. It also has holes in the top for ventilation.

I was quizzed on all of those uniform components, as well as the classic chain of command in the kitchen. It is organized in what is called the Brigade de Cuisine, or Kitchen Brigade. This was originally devised by Georges Auguste Escoffier. He was a French chef that lived from 1846 to 1935, and was responsible for establishing the order that we currently use in restaurant service, as well as many other aspects we still use in the modern kitchen.

In the interest of time, I have shortened the brigade into what is typically seen in kitchens today. At the helm is the Executive Chef, or Chef de Cuisine. The word *chef* in French means "Chief" and cuisine means "cooking." He or she is the "Chief of Cooking." This person is responsible for menu writing and the general culinary image of the restaurant. He also keeps a close handle on controlling costs. Below him is the Sous Chef (soo chef). The word sous means "under" in French. The "under" chef is responsible for making sure all of the day-to-day operations are carried out in an efficient manner. He or she is charged with managing the Chefs de Partie. These are the cooks for each station. They are the skilled technicians that actually prepare your food.

In a multi-outlet operation such as the Hyatt you will find a separate Sous Chef over each department of the kitchen and a staff of chefs de partie for each. We had a separate Banquet department led by the Banquet Chef (one of the sous chefs) and staffed by banquet cooks (the chefs de partie).

We also had a Garde Manger (gar mohn-jay) department. This is the French term for the cold prep area meaning "keeper of the food." It's also the name of the person responsible for all of the cold preparations like pates, chilled soups, cheese trays, fruit trays, crudité (vegetable) trays, hors d'oeuvres, etc. We had a Garde Manger Chef in charge of these preparations and even ice carvings. He was insanely talented. Previously he had worked for an ice carving company in Orlando. Hunkered down in our large walk-in freezer, he used to chain saw, chisel, and file some awesome sculptures.

At one point, he started teaching me the basics of ice carving by having me practice on a bar of soap. I actually learned how to make a clown fish with coral growing behind it. Yes, out of a bar of soap! I remember by the age of twenty-five he had already experienced the death of a child, and he was still dealing with the immense pain. His calm demeanor was welcoming, but his eyes spoke of a deep sadness. He didn't stay for very long, as he gave in to the restlessness within. Years later I worked with a gentleman that said to me, "I always try to treat people with respect, because you never know what all they have on their plate." I couldn't agree more.

As you can see, French plays a very prominent role in the modern kitchen. This is because of something I alluded to in the previous chapter, called Culinary French, which is the official language in the professional kitchen. It doesn't mean that we go around speaking French all day while at work. There is however, an enormous amount of culinary terms which are in fact French.

Chef Darren was constantly testing me on my terminology. He also taught me some vital lessons on food safety. One of which was concerning the *temperature danger zone*. This is the range of 40°-140° in which bacteria flourishes. I learned that shocking an item doesn't only stop the carry-over cooking process, but it also allows the product to quickly pass through the temperature danger zone so bacteria doesn't have a chance to thrive.

I worked the sauté station on the cook's line in the City Center Café kitchen within the hotel. Every day was like I was in a really busy classroom with high stakes involved. There were no prep cooks here. I was responsible for all of my own prep work for the sauté station. That lesson I learned back at Shoney's about failing to plan and planning to fail was in full effect. Among all of my daily prep was a sauce called beurre rouge sauce. This literally means "red butter." It is both a *stratified* and an *emulsion* sauce. Red wine is first placed in a pot and cooked down or reduced. Afterward, heavy cream is added and reduced. Both reductions create layers or stratifications of flavor. Then the pot is pulled off the fire and whole butter is stirred into it. The butter emulsifies with the reductions and adds body and richness. It must be held at a temperature that is not too hot or else it will break. The butter itself is an emulsion of milk solids, fat, and water which will separate, causing the entire sauce to break down. It must of course, be kept at a temperature above the danger zone. We kept it in a bain marie (water bath) in the steam table. I learned that there is also a beurre blanc (white butter) sauce made with white wine instead of red.

We were making what are known as composed plates, where every item on the plate has its own separate preparation and they are juxtaposed together on the plate as one dish. It is a very intricate way of cooking, and at the time it was all new to me. Long gone were the days of being able to toss all of the ingredients in one pan, simmer and serve. Now I had to concentrate on three different pans just for one dish. I may have three, four or five of these composed plates working at one time.

My multi-tasking skills were truly being put to the test and I was growing at a rapid pace. It was literally trial by fire. As the sauté cook, I was also responsible for the special of the day. This was an awesome learning experience because I was able to take the basic concepts I was learning, and put them to creative use in each daily special. I would present it to Chef Darren which allowed my natural creativity to be grounded by technical critique. If he gave me the green light, the item would make it onto the specials board for the evening. Some nights he did the special himself and we maintained a friendly (yet competitive) contest of "Who can have the most specials sold?!" I remember he took the title for the most specials ever sold in one night. I, however, held the title for consistently selling the most specials on average.

A skill that I hadn't anticipated developing was oral presentation. By default, I had to also present my special to the wait staff each evening during our pre-service meeting. It sounds like a simple task, but when you are presenting a dish that you personally created it can be quite intimidating. Remember, I was still a twenty-one-year-old high school drop-out who was presenting my creation to the professional staff of a three-star hotel. I had to sell my concept to the wait staff, so they would sell it to the guests. There is already a full menu for the patrons to choose from so your special had better be worth it's salt. The wording you use will affect the wording the staff may choose when describing it to each table.

I was starting to draw on things I learned growing up under stern parents. My dad used to tell my brother and me, "Speak intelligibly; annunciate!" All of Chief Edwards' lessons on proper speaking etiquette were now paying off. This also helped me develop my plate presentation skills. I had to make a sample dish and it was displayed at the entrance to the dining room. Chef Darren explained to me that people eat with their eyes first. Not only does it have to sound good, it must look good, and of course, taste good.

Once again, the Lord had shown me favor and the Executive Chef also had taken a liking to me. At one point, I had given my two-week notice to quit, but both chefs let me think it over for a couple of days. They held on to it instead of turning it in to HR. I decided to stay, and the Executive Chef got rid of my typed notice.

During this season I also began practicing my craft at home. This meant staying up late into the early morning hours reading and cooking. I learned how to make a thickening agent called roux (pronounced roo). Its a one-to-one ratio (by weight) of fat to flour. A roux is used to thicken classic French sauces. However, in contemporary cooking we don't utilize roux very much as we have shifted to lighter sauces. Chefs typically now focus on reductions, relishes, coulis, purees, and so on. We'll tackle these in a moment. I just about drove Lisa insane with my new-found roux. Everything contained a roux-thickened sauce!

I did eventually move on to practicing the lighter options at home, but not before learning and practicing the five Mother (or Grand) Sauces of classic French cuisine. These are standard sauces from which many "derivative sauces" can be made.

The first is Bechamel (BEH-shuh-mel) sauce which starts with roux and has milk and nutmeg added. A derivative of Bechamel is Mornay, which contains gruyere cheese. The next is Veloute` (VEL-oo-tay). This starts with roux and has white stock (stock made from unroasted bones of any type; beef, chicken, pork, etc.). The third Mother Sauce is Hollandaise. It is an emulsion sauce in which eggs have been cooked over a double-boiler while constantly whisking. It is removed from the indirect heat source and clarified butter is slowly streamed in while vigorously whisking, and then is seasoned. As with the beurre rouge sauce, it must be held in a steam table so as not to allow it to separate. You can add a red wine-tarragon reduction to make a derivative called Bearnaise Sauce. The fourth Mother Sauce is Tomato Sauce. Sauce Tomate (the original version) is made with the addition of roux and salt pork. Today we typically forgo these two ingredients for a lighter finish. Last but certainly not least we have Sauce Espagnole (espon-YOLE), or brown sauce. Supposedly the name is because of something that happened during King Louis VIII's wedding to Anne. Her Spanish chefs felt the brown sauce needed tomatoes added for a fuller flavor. It was widely enjoyed and thus named after Spain. A major derivative is Demi-glace (dimmy-gloss) which literally means "semi-glaze." I would venture to say that demi-glace is the most widely used derivative sauce in all of French cuisine. There is probably no such thing as a restaurant serving Classic French cuisine without including a demi-glace on at least one menu item.

Moving forward, I did learn the lighter sauces of contemporary cuisine. One of which is called coulis (coo-LEE). It is typically a sweet preparation in which berries or other fruit are cooked down with sugar and a little water. The mixture is then blended and strained. If you allow the blender to run long enough to make the mixture perfectly smooth you can leave it unstrained and you have a puree. We typically think of puree as being an ingredient used within a preparation. It is, but it can also be presented as a finished sauce or condiment. Simply adjust the seasoning and be very careful not to "hammer" the ingredients. That is our term for cooking the *life* out of something. Overcooked ingredients can make a puree take on a dull color and alter the flavor. This brings up another lesson I was learning: how to use discretion. I was becoming efficient at maintaining a delicate touch concerning seasoning and cooking techniques. More isn't necessarily better!

Whew, if only I was able to carry that last lesson over into my personal life. Now we get to the reason why this chapter is titled *Squab with Duchess Potatoes, Bitter Greens and Beurre Rouge*. Squab is just the name for a young pigeon. There is a very informative website called *Pigeons for Meat* (yes, that's really the name). They offer the following explanation:

"Squab refers to a young unfledged Pigeon. In other words, a Pigeon that cannot yet fly. The word has come to refer specifically to very young Pigeons…Not QUITE baby Pigeons. Not QUITE adult Pigeons either."

The authors go on to say that the word "squab" most likely has Norwegian roots as does "squabble." Apparently, pigeons fight a lot over things like food and the best place to perch. When humans argue we are likened to immature pigeons and are described as "squabbling." At this point in our life together Lisa and I were definitely "squabs" in every sense of the word. We were spiritually too young to fly, yet rambunctious enough to indulge in some serious squabbles.

The Duchess potatoes are an elegant variation of mashed potatoes. They have egg yolks and cream added then they are decoratively piped onto a tray using a pastry bag and baked until golden brown. The cream adds richness while the egg yolks fortify them to hold their form through the baking process. They are humble yet elegant. Lisa was my duchess, my lady, my wife. She had humble beginnings, but was an elegant woman. As in the case of the squab, the bitter greens also describe us to a "T." We were very green (young and inexperienced) yet we were already growing very bitter. We were also dealing with the anguish of suffering two miscarriages by this point. She desperately wanted to have a baby, and not being able to was adding to the bitter vibes in our marriage. As an interesting side note, under-ripe produce tends to be bitter. The weathering through more seasons of growth produces smoother, sweeter characteristics.

The beurre rouge represents blood in two ways. It's a red wine sauce which can speak to the amount of blood, sweat, and many tears we shed from the beginning. I immediately found wife husbandry to be a daunting task.

Secondly, beurre rouge is a sauce and sauces are designed to cover things. Through all of our early dysfunction God was continually covering us with His grace and mercy through the Blood of Jesus. That being said I had, unfortunately, been unfaithful by this point. Later, I even moved out for a while with a so-called friend. I think one of the saving graces was that I was and still am intimidated by women. I never had any "game." In fact, Lisa was the one that approached me when we started dating years earlier.

Even though I was now not at home with my wife, I still didn't find myself in another woman's arms again through this period of time. Eventually, Lisa and one of her close friends came over with Bibles in hand and brought me back home.

There was always a lot of tension between us. On our good days we were Bonnie and Clyde; on our bad days we were oil and water. We had completely different ways of communicating. She believed in hashing everything out in the heated moment. I believed in walking away and cooling off. I thank God that one thing I did not develop was an abusive nature. I already had anger issues, but my way of dealing with it was to walk away. The problem was, I would leave and not come back until some crazy hour early the next morning. That same cycle of mischief from my childhood was still at work.

Though I was saved, I seemed to be going in circles and not growing very much spiritually. I had even been groomed for ministry at the United Methodist Church where we attended. I preached from the pulpit once a month during our Youth Sunday service. That didn't last long of course as I was unstable and fell away from church all together. Going in circles can be quite frustrating.

At one point, we drove to Atlanta to visit that same friend of hers who was now attending college. Being from Tampa, I wasn't used to driving among the Downtown Atlanta traffic. I was attempting to navigate the directions that my wife was calling out as she nervously deciphered the map. This was back in 1996 when you had to use one of those big fold-out maps to figure out where you were going. Now, we just use our GPS on the dash or on our phones. At one point, while lost in all of this downtown traffic, I accidentally got onto an onramp to the interstate. We drove for a couple of minutes and miraculously there appeared another Downtown Atlanta exit sign. But wait a minute…I thought we had just left downtown. What we found out was that the interstate formed a "beltway" around the downtown area. We were able to travel in a complete loop and not get lost. We came to take great comfort in being able to get on and back off of the interstate as we learned our way around. That four-day period was one time in our lives when we were thankful for being able to go in circles.

Sometimes God allows us to go in circles to give us another opportunity to make the correct decision. Otherwise, that chance may be lost forever, sending us down an unfamiliar stretch of road that we are not yet ready for. I have since learned to pay attention when it seems I'm going through the same seasons over and over.

As we continued to work on our relationship, my instability led me to quit the Hyatt Regency Hotel and do a very short stent at the Double Tree Hotel as a breakfast cook. This lasted for only a couple of months because I was completely allergic to getting up at 4:40 a.m., and at work by 5:30 a.m. every morning.

I quickly found another job at Tia's Tex Mex Cantina and HATED that job! I started as a prep cook, and soon moved to evening line cook. The problem was, after being exposed to three-star cuisine I couldn't appreciate where I was. I had become a food snob and constantly had this feeling of being behind the eight ball. It seemed like I was always starting over and wasn't where I should be, or needed to be, in my career. I was tirelessly studying and practicing, never being satisfied. For the rest of my culinary career I would be driven by an inner restlessness which led to many, many sleepless nights.

I was at Tia's for about a month and couldn't take it any longer. One day, my wife and I drove to Romano's Macaroni Grill which was within walking distance from Tia's. Dressed in a crisp white shirt and tie I went inside and asked for an application. Upon filling it out, I patiently waited for the manager so I could interview with him and leave a resume. I waited... and waited... and waited. My wife and I were very old school, so she was sitting outside in the hot car all of this time because we didn't think it professional to show up for an interview accompanied by a guest. After a while, I got frustrated and discouraged. I went outside, got behind the wheel, and cranked the car up. Immediately, Lisa asked me how it went. I told her that it didn't go at all. She then just looked at me, smiled and said, "Go get your job." I paused for a moment, turned the car off, went back in, and asked again to speak with the manager. A while later, I came back out to the car as a new Macaroni Grill employee!

I started as a grill cook and soon the Executive Chef and I began butting heads. But it was kind of one of those, "too much alike" scenarios. We actually had a mutual respect for each other's professional abilities. He eventually recommended me for a promotion. I was put in touch with the Area Manager for the Virginia-Carolina Region. He and I spoke over the phone and arranged a meeting in Carey, North Carolina. I didn't want to take many days off of work, so Lisa and I packed a few things and trusted God to help us find a place to stay during a weekend excursion. We were also trusting God that our '89 Ford Thunderbird would make it there and back. It was a beautiful city and we were already envisioning ourselves living there.

When I reported to the restaurant on that Saturday for my interview with the Area Manager, the staff said he wasn't there. The manager had me wait while he tried to track him down on his cell phone. Eventually, he caught up with him. It turns out we had a miscommunication, because he wasn't even in the state. He was in Virginia. Whew talk about irate! I was fit to be tied, but I maintained my composure. Lisa and I drove back home to Tampa the next day and licked our wounds. My anger had been kindled and at work it was hard for me not to show it. But God was, and still is, on the throne. A new location was slated to open in South Florida and my General Manager recommended me for a Sous Chef position. About two months later I was in the management training program to prepare me for my new job. After my training we were relocated to Pembroke Pines, Florida which is just west of Hollywood and northwest of Miami. A team of us were going to be opening this new location. I was thinking, "Finally, my big break." Not only was I now moving up the ranks of the Brigade, I was also going to a region where fine cuisine had more prominence. And to think just months earlier I had almost walked out on my blessing…literally. If my wife hadn't encouraged me that day when we were sitting outside of Macaroni Grill with the car running, I would have driven off from my future.

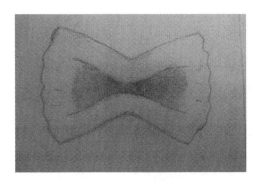

"Come con la farfalle, la fine e` a volte solo l'inizio…
"As with the butterfly, sometimes the end is just the beginning."

~JSE

Chapter 6:

~WOOD-FIRED SOCKEYE SALMON WITH PAPAYA SLAW, FARFALLE, LIME-CILANTRO BUTTER AND MOJO SAUCE~

T he title of this chapter seems long and complicated, which is for good reason…it is! Around this time (the late 1990's) the names of composed plates on high-end menus had become like run-on sentences. The industry has since gone away from that trend and simplified the verbage a little. This menu item represents the complex, multi-layered cooking I would study and practice during this phase of my career. It also speaks to the fact that, now living in the region known as South Florida, my cooking took on a distinct shift in style, as there was a distinct shift of influence.

The wood-firing of the salmon leads us into my new position upon arriving in South Florida, as it was certainly a trial by fire. It was early 1997 and Lisa and I had loaded up our Ryder truck with the car in tow on a trailer, and ventured south into the great unknown. The specific date was January 18, 1997, which I remember because my mom and Lisa's dad share that birthday. After making the four hour trip we landed in a brave new world that would forever shape us. We hit the ground running, and I mean we *really* hit the ground running. It was Saturday afternoon when we got to Pembroke Pines. No time to unpack though because I had an orientation to attend, where all of us managers were to welcome the new staff. The restaurant was set to open in a few days and there was much work to do. I literally pulled the moving truck right into the restaurant parking lot after exiting the highway. The car was even still on the trailer hitched to the back. Lisa joined us during the orientation and she got a chance to meet the other managers, employees, and corporate trainers who were there to guide us through the first few weeks. After the orientation, we drove to our new apartment and began unloading the truck. Once everything was unloaded, I had only one all-important task left to do before the night was over. Everything else could wait until we had both the time and energy, except for putting that bed together. Above all else, we were in desperate need of a good night's sleep. On Sunday we took a day of rest as we prepared ourselves for the road ahead. The next morning I reported for my first day as a Sous chef. I was anxious, excited, and humbled all rolled into one. I also remember feeling blessed, because at the age of twenty-three I was now going to be making a salary of $28,000 per year with an average fifty-five hour work week. That was big money to a high school drop-out who was still managing to keep everybody fooled. Just five years earlier I was sleeping on the bathroom floor of an empty house after having spent two weeks in jail, with seemingly no prospects for my future.

During that first week Lisa was at home unpacking boxes and putting things in their rightful place, while I was actually doing the same thing at work. We had to unpack the kitchen equipment and utensils, all of which was shrink wrapped and sitting in the middle of the restaurant's sparkling, new kitchen. Then we had to receive and put away all of our food deliveries, which arrived over the next couple of days. Talk about a lot of product. We had to stock our entire supply of dry goods, refrigerated goods, frozen goods, paper, and plastic items, so on and so forth. Whew, I was just ready to start cooking! The front of the house staff was also going through all of their pre-opening rituals.

The second week began with us prepping our mise en place (mees-ohn-plohs). This is the culinary French term meaning "everything in it's place." It is when you have gathered and processed all of your ingredients in preparation for putting together a particular dish. Our brigade was made up of one Executive chef, two Sous chefs, the prep cooks, line cooks and the dish washers. It was a huge learning curve for our executive chef and us sous chefs to properly train the staff on all things Macaroni Grill. The corporate trainers were worth their weight in gold. They were our eyes, ears and hands through the entire process.

That week also brought what is known as a soft opening. This was where we invited all of the family and friends of the employees to dine in the restaurant, but we didn't advertise being open. The rule was that if any members of the general public came in because they thought we were open, then we would try out our chops on them. The servers explained to them that we were having a soft opening and they were welcome guests as we practiced our craft. Looking back, I think it's an interesting business strategy because it allows you to work out a lot of the kinks while serving a more forgiving clientele, and still generate revenue.

That second and third week I greatly exceeded the fifty-five hours per week stipulated in my contract. I ended up working eighty hours during week two and about seventy-six hours during week three. I was like a zombie each night when I got home. I did, however, go on to learn so many lessons in that first management position that I can't possibly number them all. I will say this: the overwhelming majority of those lessons were about people not food. I was really learning how to help lead a team to victory on a daily basis.

One of the most profound moments I can remember was when one of the assistant managers was talking to me about how to manage employees. He said, "Build them up, tear them down and build them up again." He was one of the hardest working and non-relenting managers I have ever seen even to this day. A very "in-your-face" kind of person, but as hard-driving as he was, he always started each shift with a pep rally of sorts. He would always greet you with an upbeat motivational word. Then as the shift got under way he would press that accelerator and start demanding a million things at once. He pushed the entire kitchen staff (including us chefs) very hard the whole night. Other managers were less vocal and seemingly less demanding. Interestingly though, he was the *only* one that would bless you at the end of the night before you went home. He made it a point to give an encouraging word as each of us headed out the door. He was not a practicing Christian, but I believe he got that lesson correct. Now, he definitely used some choice words during the "tear them down" portion of the formula, but the overall point was well taken.

A serious lesson in humility was also in store. During my previous seasons as a dishwasher, I had never run the dish pit by myself as many times as I did while a sous chef at Macaroni Grill. We would have very strict goals for our numbers each day. Labor and food cost were the two biggies in the kitchen. There were many times when I had to send the dish guys home and finish their job at the end of the night because we were in danger of going over our projected labor cost for the day. I found that the higher you want to travel on the ladder of success, the lower you must first travel. I also became aware of the fact that if I wanted to build and lead a successful team, I needed to serve my employees. Sounds kind of familiar; *"He who would be chief among you, let him serve"* (Matt 20:27). It was good to expect excellence from them, so long as I had served them with the proper tools to produce excellence. Over those two years in that position, serving would take the form of everything from providing teachable moments, to going to bat for an employee in need, to imposing strict guidelines when necessary, to working side-by-side in the trenches, to simply praying for them at times.

For some of them I had become a mentor of sorts. We had hired a few guys that were completing the final stage of their incarceration by living in a halfway house while maintaining gainful employment. I was invited to come and speak at an event they were having at one point. Nervously, I agreed and turned to the only material I was prepared to cover...The Holy Bible. I was kind of hesitant though, because it wasn't a Christian event per se. I was nervous enough about public speaking, let alone speaking about the Bible in a non-Christian setting to a group of ex-cons. Doubt started to set in as I thought, "These guys are *not* going to want to hear this." I went with it nonetheless because it was the only material I had prepared. When I arrived at the halfway house that evening, I sat my Bible down so I could sign-in. The lady checking me in said, "Oh, you're bringing the Word too?!" It was a subtle affirmation and I was immediately calmed. Of the three speakers that night, all of us ended up "bringing The Word."

One of the types of pasta we served at Macaroni Grill was farfalle (far-fah-lay). It means butterfly in Italian but we in America know it as bowtie pasta. This job was my springboard into effectively managing people. Through that experience, I had entered the cocoon of hard knocks and emerged ready to spread my wings and fly.

During that two-year period I also started studying specific chefs for the first time in my career. I went to Barnes and Noble and read everything I could find about the Louisiana mega chef, Paul Prudhomme. He had such an awesome way of explaining food concepts. By then he had written several books and I perused them all. My two favorites were *Chef Paul Prudhomme's Louisiana Kitchen (1984)* and *Chef Paul Prudhomme's Seasoned America (1991)*. I will never forget the first recipe of his I learned was scratch cornbread using corn masa. I had memorized the recipe and then gone home and written it down. When I made it, I was blown away by the infinitely fresh corn aroma wafting through our two-bedroom apartment. To this day I am a fool for authentic tacos made with fresh, soft corn tortillas. When I make my own at home, I lightly toast the corn tortillas before making the tacos…insanely good! From *Chef Paul Prudhomme's Seasoned America* I learned how to make some serious black beans that I must say are my favorite recipe out of any black beans I've ever eaten. They say you're in trouble when you love your own cooking. I can agree. I gained a lot of weight over those couple of years just from cooking and eating in the wee hours after long days at work. Unfortunately, I brought Lisa down that road with me. She was my guinea pig as I tested, tasted, and goaded her into tasting. I even adapted my first biscuit recipe from his "Mama's Yeast Rolls" recipe in *Seasoned America*. Sadly the culinary world lost Chef Paul on October 8, 2015 and of all the chefs I've ever studied he is the one I most regret not being able to meet. His wonderful demeanor made him a well-loved chef the world over.

While working for Romano's Macaroni Grill I learned an indispensable amount of structured business practices and how the two biggies (food cost and labor cost) affect the bottom line in a restaurant. During shifts when I was the opening chef, I was responsible for creating and costing-out the lunch special of the day. I was also responsible for creating a labor pro forma for the kitchen staff based on the projected daily revenue.

Interestingly though, despite all of the business lessons, I continued to hunger for more complex and diverse cuisine. This led me to once again, continue looking for jobs that would be more challenging on a culinary level. I applied at *Mark's Las Olas,* which was Chef Mark Militello's flagship operation. Las Olas ("The Waves" in Spanish) is a very popular street in Fort Lauderdale which runs from downtown all the way to the beach. Chef Mark was one of a group of chefs that were referred to as the *Mango Gang.* These guys put South Florida cooking on the map, as they gave it national distinction in the world of food. I applied for a position there, which also included a written culinary quiz. I didn't know as much as I thought I knew and thus, didn't get the job. But I was on the hunt.

Soon I ended up seeing an ad in the Herald Tribune for a Sous chef position at a restaurant called *Norman's.* It was in Coral Gables, which is the district of Miami where the University of Miami is located. The restaurant was owned by Norman Van Aken and I had no earthly idea who he was. I researched him a little and found out he was also a member of the *Mango Gang.* As a matter of fact, he was dubbed the "Founding Father" of what is known as New World Cuisine. It is a vibrant cuisine that encompasses Latin, Asian, African and American Southern flavors with classic French techniques. I researched further and found out that he had been awarded Best Chef in the Southeastern Region of the US in 1997. I was in awe.

I got my resume together and applied for their Sous chef position. On a quiet afternoon, I sat in the empty dining room prior to the start of dinner service and filled out an application. After a while, I noticed a gentleman sitting at the bar talking to a woman about his upcoming itinerary. All of a sudden I was frozen as I thought...THAT'S HIM, THAT'S HIM! It was Chef Norman himself as I recognized him from photos. I was immediately nervous and awestruck. Not because he was a celebrity chef; I didn't know him as a celebrity. I was humbled by his accomplishments.

He had created an entire cuisine that had garnered international attention.

The thing that made it even more awe-inspiring to me was that he had never set foot in culinary school. He worked his way up and even did odd jobs at times, like being a carnival worker and a construction worker. Now he was traveling the world informing others about the diversity found in a region, in a cuisine, and in a people. He had even received an honorary doctorate degree from Johnson and Wales University, which is one of the top culinary schools in the nation. He lectured at their North Miami Beach campus regularly. All of this, coming from a guy that had no formal culinary education, just an absolute zeal for learning and a tremendous work ethic. He read everything he could get his hands on and worked tirelessly in many kitchens across the country. His story truly spoke to me.

Here I was now, sitting in the epicenter of his genius. I left my resume and application with the bartender. Of course I never heard back from anyone, and didn't get the job, which was no surprise because I was ridiculously under-qualified. I really enjoyed the moment though. It was my first time being in a four-star restaurant and the entire experience just further fueled my passion.

Unfortunately, my personal life was becoming extremely unbalanced. Lisa and I were not doing well. Dreams of culinary success were driving me into complete unrest. That feeling of being behind the eight ball was controlling me. I was never satisfied with my current station. I had to have more; more knowledge, more success, more notoriety. This leads us into why I chose Sockeye Salmon as the protein for this chapter's title.

It is a variety of Alaskan Salmon that makes the dangerous and taxing trip upstream once a year to its breeding ground. As they swim northward, they not only have to overcome the southward flowing current, but then there are also the bears. These beasts wade into the water and attempt to catch sockeye leaping out of the water to conquer the rushing falls. It seemed as though I was forever fighting against the current of age and time, while also dodging the clutches of grizzly self-doubt.

My restlessness soon led me to land a job at Weston Hills Country Club. It was located in Weston which is just north of Pembroke Pines and west of Fort Lauderdale. I had never worked at a country club before so it was a new experience. As usual I took a cut in pay from my previous job for a better learning opportunity. This seemed to be a theme where I would make what resembled a backward step in order to hopefully follow it with a leap forward. So far this technique had served me well. Lisa was however, a bit tired of the uncertainty every couple of years. I asked her to trust me on this one and she did.

Weston Hills was another multi-outlet facility which reminded me of the Hyatt Regency Hotel back in Tampa. We had a Banquet department and a Garde Mange department. There was also a members-only restaurant called *The Grille Room*. It was basically a fully functioning restaurant with it's own prep kitchen, walk-in refrigerator, cook's line, walk-up window for golfers, and large dining room. There was a nice dark wood and granite bar in the middle of the dining room that served as a gathering place for regulars and golfers returning from the links. We also had beverage cart service for golfers out on the course and a satellite take-out operation between the ninth and tenth holes. This was like a high end rest stop between the "front nine" and the "back nine." Golfers could stop off and use the restroom while getting some refreshments and take a break from the blistering South Florida sun.

Our brigade was under the leadership of the Executive Chef who was a very cool German named Dieter Wenninger (Vin-in-ger). When I started at Weston there was only one Sous chef, whose name was David (his last name escapes me). This was a monumental operation for just two managing chefs. About a month after I started as a chef de partie in *The Grille Room*, Chef David put in his notice. He was offered a job that he had applied for before starting at Weston Hills.

The management decided to replace him with two separate Sous chefs. One would be over Banquets and Garde Manger, while the other would be over *The Grille Room* and the food/beverage outlets on the course. Again God smiled on me and Chef David had taken a liking to me. He told me to apply for the *Grille Room* Sous position. He even put in a word with Chef Dieter, The Food and Beverage Director (Dieter's boss), and the General Manager. Man, talk about favor. He liked my work ethic and my passion.

I had to write a sample menu and submit it for review by Chef David and Chef Dieter, along with my resume. I wound up getting the job, which really was a blessing considering I had only been there for a couple of months. The banquet sous chef position went to someone from the outside, even though the lead banquet cook had been there for several years. They were apparently looking to change directions. I came face to face with *that* fact very soon after taking the *Grille Room* Sous position.

The Food and Beverage Director (Edward) quickly approached me with the task of writing a new menu for the restaurant. I had to write it and roll-out samples of each dish. Once Edward critiqued and approved it, I had to train all of the kitchen staff on how to prepare and present the items. In addition, I had to teach the wait staff about each new item and allow them to taste them. Oh, did I mention I was twenty-five years old at this point and was now managing kitchen staff in their thirties, forties, fifties and even a chef in his sixties? And yes, they all had worked there for several years and were set in their ways. Yikes! Talk about the challenge of swimming upstream. They were however, a great group, they truly were.

The executive chef hired a young lady from Venezuela to take-over my vacated line position. That was definitely a gift, because she was actually younger than me and had not too long ago graduated from culinary school. She was fresh, impressionable and full of ideas while remaining receptive to critique. The first time we met was actually an awkward moment. I was in the banquet chef's office doing computer work while munching on a snack. Just then Chef Dieter brought her in to meet me. I was trying to chew and swallow while wiping my mouth with the left hand and attempting a hand shake with my right. Between chewing, I muddled out something like, "Hi, nice to meet you." She just shook my hand and gave a reserved smile as if to say, "This guy seems like a real chump. I hope I didn't make a mistake coming to work here." There's nothing like meeting another professional for the first time with your mouth stuffed full of food.

In time, we actually made a good team. She worked the sauté station, which was responsible for the special of the day. Each day, we would confer over the components and presentation. It was truly reminiscent of the Hyatt, only I was now Chef Darin and she was "Little John."

Though Chef Dieter was my direct supervisor, I found myself being developed very heavily by *his* boss, Edward. Beyond the initial task of creating and implementing the new menu, he went on to continually give me new assignments. One of which was to have a feature dessert every Friday night and Saturday night. This was a huge learning curve, because in all of my experience thus far, desserts were uncharted territory for me.

As with the other phases of my career, I learned far too many things to cover in this chapter. What I will say is this position was like a combination of The Hyatt Regency Hotel and Romano's

Macaroni Grill. I learned how to take raw culinary ideas and put them into functional practice, as in the Hyatt experience. At the same time, I learned how to successfully lead a team to victory, as in the Macaroni Grill experience.

During this time, Lisa had started working in a Chiropractor's office. It was a small operation in which there was only one doctor providing clinical care, with his wife managing the business aspects. They had a small staff of two women working in the morning and two women working in the evening. This doctor was a beast. He was completely sold on the benefits of Chiropractics, and it showed.

He would start with 6:30 a.m. appointments, see patients all morning, take a nap in his office during lunch, and treat patients all afternoon and into the evening until about 8pm. He also did all of the x-rays for each new patient right there in the office. Because it was such a small operation, they didn't offer health insurance coverage. They did offer free Chiropractic services for the employees and their families. Once again, that meant the doctor himself also treated all of the employees and their family members. Talk about thorough.

When I came in for my consultation, he had me sit down and watch an educational video about the science of chiropractic medicine, and how it works to use the body's own physiology to restore function and relieve pain. Then he did my one-on-one interview in his office, followed by x-rays. Upon my next visit, he went over my x-rays with me, and started my treatments. He did this with all of his patients, employees and their families. It's a shame that so many quacks have given that profession a bad name, but I am very thankful that my first and only exposure to it was in dealing with an absolute professional. To this day, I am a huge advocate of Chiropractics when done correctly.

It was also during this time that our relationship continued to deteriorate. Now that she was making an income, Lisa even started looking for apartments for rent. The doctor and his wife had let her take on the housekeeping duties at the office for extra income, should she move forward with getting her own place. Though I was learning a lot professionally, I was continually unsatisfied with life. Being married didn't matter, because I was still supremely lonely, not being able to relate to her or any of my peers. I would have periodic episodes of staying out all night by myself drinking. On one instance, I had the day off from work and Lisa didn't get off until about 9pm. I went out and never came to get her from work that night. Neither of us had a cell phone, so she couldn't call me to find out what happened. She had to catch a ride home from a young lady working at the Subway sandwich shop next to their office. I ended up making it home sometime early the next morning.

The problem with being a loner is that you can't remove the bad influences from around you. They are within. You're your own worst enemy, and there's no one else to blame. Lisa eventually moved back to Tampa and stayed with her parents for a while. After some soul searching on both ends, we decided to give it another go and she came home. Neither one of us really wanted to be divorced, so we drew close and decided to try and make it work.

In about September of 1999, Lisa's boss took a trip out of town for a medical convention. When he returned, I had an appointment scheduled with him for a chiropractic treatment. When he came into the treatment room he handed me a business card. It was a thick, high quality card of solid black background with white writing. I glanced down at it and then did a double take. It was the business card of the Chef de Cuisine at *Norman's*.

During the flight back to Miami, the Doctor had struck up a conversation with a gentleman sitting next to him. He just happened to be the chef de cuisine at *Norman's*. The doctor remembered Lisa telling him how enthralled I was with Norman Van Aken's cuisine. He told the chef about me and got his business card. The chef told him to have me call ASAP, because they had a guy leaving soon and needed to replace him. Whaaaaaaat?!!! I was floating on cloud nine when he handed me that card. We had just eaten there in August. Lisa had taken me for my birthday the last two years in a row. On the first occasion we met Chef Norman briefly while he was walking around in the dining room greeting tables. I thought that was such a nice touch for a star chef to be walking around speaking to the patrons. When he approached our table, I remember him saying, "Welcome, glad to have you." Of course, I got nervous and said something super stupid like, "We're glad we could be here!" It's all good.

The following year, I bought his latest book at the time, while we were there dining. I now had all three of his books, which I avidly read, or should I say, studied. At my earliest convenience, I called the chef de cuisine and we scheduled an evening for me to come in and do a *stage* (stohj). This is a practice where you work a shift, or several shifts, without pay. The idea is for you to get a feel for the operation, while the operation gets a feel for you. In the old school, chefs did days-long and even weeks-long stages at top restaurants to gain valuable experience in places where there were no available job openings. It is still a way chefs get their foot in the door at high-end places where openings are hard to come by.

The things I saw during that evening made my head spin. I was like, "We are *definitely* not in Kansas anymore Toto." At the end of the night they offered me a job. It was a moment that signaled a shift in the universe. My entire career had been spent doing one thing while looking ahead to the next. There was always a discrepancy between where I was, and where I wanted to be; cooking one type of cuisine, while trying desperately to emulate another. I was now about to enter a place where I had no vision beyond it. It was that clearing in the woods after vigorously searching through the night for so long. When day break hit and I found myself in the very place for which I had been searching, I just was in awe. I had actually managed to get around the eight ball. For the first time I wasn't taking a "stepping stone" position. I was finally "in the house", and it was time to dig-in and make this house my home.

I was assigned to work Garde Manger which was the cold prep station. Now, that is about as understated as a thing can get. First, let's tackle the mise en place. There were no prep cooks, besides one young lady that prepped some specific items and that was it. The entire prep for my station was up to me, as with the Hyatt experience. The difference was that at the Hyatt, I had about two hours of mise en place for my station before service. At *Norman's* I arrived at work between 11 am and 12pm to prep all of my mise en place for 5:30pm service. I would spend as many hours prepping mise en place as I would actually pushing-out food during service.

Remember, prep work was my weakness, which was okay, because I was about to get an insane dose of encouragement in this area. All of my items had to be prepared and kept track of. If I saw I was running low on something, then the next day that item needed to be at the top on my list of prep.

Probably the single most dreaded item I had to keep up with was the Vietnamese soft spring rolls. They were the main character in the dish entitled *Vietnamese Soft Spring Rolls with Rare Tuna Petals, Paw Paw Slaw, and Ponzu Dipping Sauce.* So let's first break down the spring rolls. They were rice paper wrappers filled with shiitake mushrooms, carrots and somen noodles. The shiitake mushrooms had to be cleaned and julienned by hand. The carrots were julienned on a mandolin, which allowed for a uniform cut. They were then marinated in mirin (sweet sake vinegar) and fresh cilantro. The somen noodles were cooked al dente, cooled, and marinated. I am unable to recall exactly what that marinade consisted of, but I believe it contained sweet Thai chili sauce and soy sauce. Everything had to be immaculately processed. The cilantro was to be chopped fine with absolutely no stems. The mushrooms had to be sautéed quickly in a very hot pan, so as not to absorb the oil and become mushy. They were then removed from the pan and laid out on a sheet tray in the refrigerator to stop the carry-over cooking. A perfectly butchered log of tuna was seasoned and seared on all sides in a smoking hot pan then removed and stored in the refrigerator to maintain it's rare temperature.

To assemble the rolls I arranged the items in an assembly line starting with a bowl of cold water. I dipped a sheet of the dry (and very brittle) rice paper into the water and moved it around until softened. Then I removed it before becoming too soft to roll without tearing and laid it out on the stainless steel counter. Next I put on a liberal portion of noodles followed by shiitakes and carrots. Now comes the moment of skill, precision and extreme patience. Taking one end of the wrapper I proceeded to roll and tuck making sure not to tear it while neatly encapsulating all of the ingredients. The finished product had to be rolled very tightly; otherwise, when cut in half it would look saggy and unkempt. Everything had to be what we called soigné (swohn-yay), which is to say, elegantly dressed or articulately styled. This took lots of practice, which was fine because we sold a lot of these so I prepped quite a few. It was a very popular item and was also on our catering menu for private parties. I remember one day, I had to prep seventy of those bad boys. OMG! My whole body hurt after prepping just that one menu item.

Next, we move on to the "Paw Paw" Slaw. Paw paw is a fruit that is largely grown in the northeastern part of North

America. It's also a loosely used term for papaya of which there are about forty-five species typically grown in South America, The West Indies, Hawaii and India. The paw paw in this dish refers to the latter, hence my inclusion of papaya slaw in the title of this chapter. We used large green papaya for it's firm texture, which held up nicely when marinated. I believe it included apple and carrots, along with some type of light vinaigrette. Again, the details are elusive.

There was also the ponzu dipping sauce. Ponzu is a Japanese dipping sauce about as common to Japanese cuisine as vinaigrette is to American cuisine. The basic components are soy sauce, citrus and mirin. I don't remember all of the other ingredients we used but I know we added ginger. All of this mise en place was just for one dish. I had several of these composed plates that I was responsible for prepping.

Plating each dish during service at *Norman's* was probably the hardest part of a job I have ever had. Because they were composed plates, serving one dish meant making a hundred moves. And *everything* was high and tight. If it was not soigné, it was not leaving the kitchen. As for the spring rolls, they had to be cut in half on the bias (at a 45 degree angle) and placed standing up at one end of a rectangular plate. The slaw was neatly mounded in the middle of the plate with not one member out of place. The rare tuna was sliced so thin that the sous chef had to be able to see through it when held up to the light. The seared edges of each rare tuna "petal" couldn't be cracked. And under no circumstance could it be over-cooked. These "petals" were then fanned out on the edge of the small mound of slaw. The ponzu was put into a square shot glass and positioned at the other end of the plate.

Chef Norman had a rule that absolutely nothing touched the rim of the plate. There were no smudges of slaw vinaigrette or droplets of ponzu on the plate. Now, this had to be done while moving at two hundred miles per hour! At *Norman's*, attention to detail was on a steroidal level.

On a different dish, I was responsible for making a sour orange mojo sauce. Mojo is a Spanish sauce whose name is taken from *mojar* which means to wet. It's a light sauce that is made largely of oil, garlic, an acid and whatever flavoring you desire. Ours was sour orange, which is a very prevalent fruit here in Florida. A couple of sour orange trees even used to grow in Lisa's parents' front yard back in Tampa. It contained a lot of garlic which had to be hand chopped. Every single clove of garlic had to be split in half lengthwise and the little green shoot had to be removed. Before that I didn't even realize that green shoot was in a garlic clove. If they remained they would result in the sauce taking on a slightly green hue. However slight the greening affect, the Sous chefs could pick-up on it right away…which meant so would Chef Norman. I won't go into all the other plates I was responsible for, but you get the picture.

It was also interesting to note the things that were *not* present in the *Norman's* kitchen. At every restaurant I had ever worked in, there were always tomatoes kept in the walk-in refrigerator. At *Norman's*, we had no tomatoes in the cooler. As a matter of fact we had no common varieties like Vine Ripes or Romas or Beef Steaks even in the building. We did have miniature heirlooms of all different types. Heirloom vegetables are ones that have been grown from unaltered seeds. All tomatoes today are from seeds that have been genetically modified for increased size or increased shelf life to accommodate our insatiable consumer appetite. Unfortunately, taste and texture suffer in the process.

We kept the heirloom tomatoes on a "ripening rack" in the corner of the kitchen. They never made it into the cooler, and were allowed to naturally ripen in a temperate area of the kitchen. Refrigeration slows the aging process hence my always finding tomatoes in the cooler at other restaurants. On the ripening rack, they aged quicker and were used quicker. This allowed us to receive very fresh heirloom deliveries on a daily basis. Another item we didn't have was mashed potatoes, or at least not the way I was used to seeing them. There was one dish on the menu that included mashed potatoes though. The cook that had it had to make them a la minute (ah-lah-minoot); in other words, to order. He had to pre-bake potatoes and hold them hot on his station. When an order came in, he put them into a metal bowl along with the seasoning and whatever other ingredients it called for, then processed them by hand with a hand masher. Whew! I was so glad that wasn't part of my station.

One night we had someone request whipped cream for some reason. We didn't offer whipped cream on the menu, so it had to be made a la minute. Okay, that's no big deal. You just take heavy whipping cream and put it in the mixer with some powdered sugar and vanilla. Turn it on medium until it thickens some and turn it up to high after its thick enough not to splash out of the bowl. After a few moments, voila! You have whipped cream. There was only one problem with this whole scenario. The mixer was in the dessert kitchen and they were too busy to make it.

The Sous chef told me to grab some heavy cream, a metal bowl, and wire whisk. I had to go into the walk-in freezer and start whipping. I was literally breathing heavily by the time I finished but in a matter of minutes I emerged from the frosty depths of the freezer with fresh whipped cream in hand. I used a balloon whisk which has wider spaces between it's thinner and more flexible wire loops. Your hand motion is amplified by the increased motion of the loops as you move the whisk back and forth at a high rate of speed. This allows for more air to be incorporated into the cream at a faster rate. A stiffer whisk would mean you would have to increase your arm and wrist motion for a longer period of time.

Your arm would basically feel like you've been pitching nine straight innings.

We were open Monday through Saturday, so everybody worked six days a week. All of the kitchen staff was on salary so as not to accrue overtime. I was making a cool $25,000 yearly salary for about seventy hours of work per week. I got yelled at more than I ever had before, or since, in my entire life. I was extremely humbled. Chef Scott (one of the two Sous chefs) yelled at me so much that my coworker who worked the station next to me started making sure I had everything ready to go for service. Even he was tired of hearing Chef Scott screaming at me. It was absolutely the most humbling experience I have ever faced. There was no more pride left in me by the end of each shift.

It's been said that we do many things in this life because of nostalgia. I think that's why to this day one of my favorite beers is Rolling Rock. Yes, I did say that as a Christian, I drink beer. This is a testimonial book, not a book of dead religion and vain repetition. The truth of the matter is, I am accustomed to drinking a beer or two at the end of my day, as I did for so many years while cooking.

At *Norman's*, the closing of the doors each night would signal a change in venue. In the kitchen, the boom box would get cranked up and they would bring out a huge plastic container we called a Lexan. It was filled with bottles of Rolling Rock floating in ice water. Each member of the kitchen brigade had two ice cold ones at his or her disposal. We would burn so many calories during a shift that, even though every night I ended with two beers, I still lost about ten pounds the first month. Once I got home I would take a shower and go straight to bed. I didn't sleep very well most nights because I was dreaming about work. It was always the same scenario that I was trailing food and the Sous chef was yelling expletives at me. I always had the same basic dream that I was horribly in the weeds and was unable to dig myself out.

On top of the physical stress, the job was kind of a logistical strain. Lisa and I only had one car and the restaurant was a forty-five-minute drive one way. If she needed the car, it would be four trips total by the time the night was over. There were many days when I asked myself why I took a $7,000 a year pay-cut to endure such misery.

The truth of the matter is that I was learning more each day than I can possibly even explain. I was also now on the "world stage" as I like to call it. It wasn't rated the number one restaurant in the country; but surviving this job would basically mean I could get a job anywhere I wanted in the country. There was no other restaurant in the Southeastern United States that could compete. The exposure was part of our salary. I had access to a modern day legend. When he wasn't out of town at an event, he was actually in the restaurant. While he was an extreme perfectionist, he was also very down-to-earth. Earlier in the day he would walk through the kitchen in jeans and a casual shirt and chit chat with us. He knew all of us by name.

I also would potentially travel with Chef Norman as he participated in different events around the country. Each time he had an event we would have a prep list of things that correlated to each station. So whatever dishes he was responsible for at the event, we would have that much more time spent producing mise en place ahead of time. For instance, let's say he was serving his *Yucca-Stuffed Shrimp with Sour Orange Mojo* during an event. I would have the sour orange mojo on my prep list because of how much time it takes to prepare. Absolutely no green garlic shoots! We had a commercial-size cryo-vac machine in the kitchen so we bagged and vacuum sealed all of the prepped items. The Sous chefs then air shipped it all to the location to meet Chef Norman. Each kitchen member was on a rotating schedule with one Sous chef to accompany him at an event. So sooner or later, I was going to be scheduled to attend one of his trips. This meant that I would be among a "League of Extraordinary Gentlemen" if you will. Each of these culinary events around the country boasts a "Who's Who" of culinary masters in their own rite.

After about a month of getting my butt handed to me, I started getting the hang of it. One day it finally just clicked. I was firing on all cylinders. Chef Scott and Chef Bryan (the other sous) even commented on the fact that I was now cooking with fire. At the end of that week, I was completely exhausted. Saturday night I got home, took a shower, and fell into the bed. Sometime during the early morning hours, Lisa woke me up and said she had been feeling very sick and wanted me to take her to the hospital. I was so out of it I actually told her I was too tired and she would have to drive herself. The whole conversation is completely a blur as I try to recall it. I immediately fell back asleep. A couple of hours later (which seemed like minutes to me) she came into the room and woke me up after returning from the hospital. I don't remember anything about that moment other than the fact that she said, "I'm pregnant." That was most definitely another "Whaaaat?!" moment.

That Sunday brought a lot of plotting and planning. It was a time of mixed emotions. I was extremely happy yet it was like the stress-o-meter had just gotten cranked-up to OMG! There were two major issues. The first was that at Norman's we didn't have health insurance. The other was that we were already barely making it financially, and now there would be an entirely new set of expenses as the family grew. I remember thinking that both of these issues would be different if she had just gotten pregnant about five weeks earlier.

At Weston Hills I was making $32,000/year with major medical insurance, vacation time, sick time and FMLA time. Now all of that was gone although, God was still in control. We looked into the COBRA coverage, but it was $500 a month with an insane deductible and copayments per visit. After another trip to the ER, she was placed on light duty; so I asked her to quit her job and focus on herself and the baby. We already had a history of miscarriage and we didn't want to take any chances. Of course this really made things tight financially. We needed to cut expenses anywhere we could. I had spoken to Chef Scott and he even got the dining room director involved in trying to locate affordable health insurance. No such luck, because back in November of 1999, pregnancy was still considered a pre-existing condition and insurance carriers could deny coverage. Thankfully, that law was eventually changed and it's no longer legal to deny coverage due to pregnancy.

Every morning we went shopping for cheaper rentals closer to the restaurant, but the search wasn't going very well. There soon came a sobering moment. We were going to have to do the unthinkable. We had fallen in love with South Florida and had planned on buying a home there. Now we were coming to the realization that it was time to move back to Tampa and live with her parents until we could get on our feet. What seemed like an awesome new beginning for us had turned into an abrupt ending. Our tour of a brave *new* world was about to become a return to the same *old* world. After not even a full three years, our gallivant was over. We already hated Tampa, and to be reduced to moving back and living under someone else's roof was a lot for both of us. Her parents were always there when we needed them but we wanted to finally spread our wings and fly.

As we planned our exit strategy I had another humbling moment. I spoke to Lisa and apologized for the situation. I had sacrificed everything for this job and it didn't pan out. By leveraging everything I actually put us in a deep hole. Then and there I promised her that I would never, ever put our family in that situation again. Leaving *Norman's* didn't hurt nearly as much as leaving our dreams for our family. We wanted to raise our children anywhere *but* Tampa.

During my final week at work Lisa packed up everything, booked our truck rental and scheduled our walkthrough with the apartment management to secure our deposit from when we moved in. She also booked our room at a hotel for our final night in South Florida because, like an idiot, I decided to work right up to our last night in town. I loaded up the truck and we slept our final night in the apartment on the floor. Lisa was set-up with the twin mattress from our guest bed for increased comfort. We woke-up and did our walkthrough and then went and checked-in at the hotel. After making sure Lisa was good, I drove the car to work and worked all night.

Chef Norman was there that night and I had all three of his books with me so he could autograph them. It really blessed me to have him address each blurb to "Chef John." I felt like a high school freshman having my yearbook signed by the most popular senior on campus. Late that night I drove to the hotel and got a few hours of sleep. The next morning we checked-out and I drove the moving truck with the car in-tow the four hours to Tampa. God was watching over us and kept us safe the whole trip. It was a very bad decision to drive on that little amount of rest but I felt I needed to work as much as possible. I had given the managers at *Norman's* the address to Lisa's parents' house to forward my final check.

As we left Pembroke Pines we were overwhelmed with sadness. I remember getting on Alligator Alley which is the part of Interstate 75 that crosses from one coast of Florida to the other. It was over. The mood in the truck was palpable; that undeniable feeling of defeat. We could feel the door on that chapter of life closing behind us as we drove into the next. What was awaiting us on this new horizon? What would life be like during this new chapter? How would we do as new parents? Only time would tell.

It had been five years, almost to the day, since I had been birthed into my pursuit of serious cuisine while working at Iavarone's in November of 1994. Interestingly enough, it is about a five-year journey between the time a Sockeye Salmon is born and when it makes the return trip to the breeding ground as an adult. The journey upstream is so physically taxing that they metabolize their outer pigment which turns them from gray to red. It's the final journey as they will breed, lay the eggs, and pass-on while their bodies provide nutrients to the ecosystem. As we made our way back upstream to Tampa, this was definitely our dying to self that we may make way for our future generation.

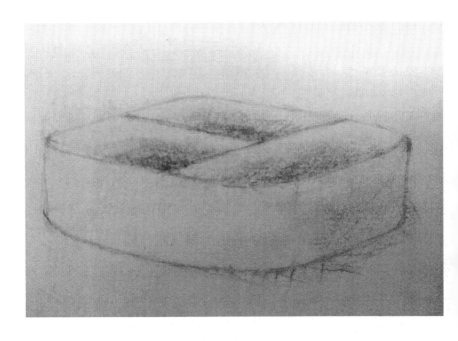

"Wisdom aids skill in the kitchen therefore, only through experience and persistence can one understand the dynamics of food."

~NME

Chapter 7:

STRAWBERRY-PEPPERCORN GLAZED BEEF *EN BENTO*
~BOILED BANANA, BRAISED GREENS, TAJINE SAUCE~

Upon arrival back in Tampa, my first order of business was to secure gainful employment. When I had spoken to Chef Norman on my final evening in Miami he told me to go to *Mise En Place Restaurant* and they would hire me. This was the only place in Tampa that he had a recommendation to try…so you know I did! Shortly after getting settled into our temporary headquarters with Lisa's parents, I got an interview with Chef Marty Blitz who is the co-owner of *Mise En Place* which serves New American Cuisine. It was the holiday season of 1999, so even though the restaurant wasn't hiring they had a very active catering business that could always use more help. I met with Ann Frechette who is still their catering director and she put me right to work.

January 1, 2000 marked five years of marriage for us. Looking back, it sounds a whole lot shorter than it felt by that point. We celebrated at home and I had actually made enough money to save up and buy Lisa a new ring because her first one had gotten lost. The pregnancy was moving along very well, and the catering gig was keeping me decently busy, but I needed something more stable. I was constantly scouring the newspaper for job leads.

Eventually, I answered an ad for a kitchen manager position at Bloomingdale Golfer's Club. Bloomingdale is a subdivision of Valrico which is southeast of the Tampa city limits. Our old high school (Bloomingdale High School) is right down the street. The golfer's club was a small and very old facility, but the Food and Beverage Director seemed extremely professional and I got a good feeling from the interview. I ended up getting the job and we later found an apartment about a seven-minute drive away. Upon accepting the new position I was nervous, as I always am when starting a new job. This time it was because even though I had been in management before, I was now the head of an entire kitchen; hence the inclusion of free-range beef in the title of this chapter. It symbolizes the fact that during this season of my career I would go on to have three jobs where I had "free-range" of the kitchen operations.

Thankfully this first job at the helm was a very small facility. There were just two cooks; one for lunch service and one for dinner service. There was only one dishwasher, who worked a swing shift between both meals. Then there was me. Our kitchen was very tiny, but man did we crank some serious food out at times. Bloomingdale Golfer's Club hosted a lot of tournaments, which meant a lot of food going out at one time. Many times, they would have a boxed lunch that they would receive before the start of play. Then they would have a meal upon their return. Sometimes it would be burgers that could be grabbed from the outdoor grill station as they finished. Other times, it was a full banquet with a buffet in the clubhouse to be enjoyed after everyone had finished and the scores were tallied.

This job proved to be less about culinary arts and much, much more about learning logistics. I was getting my first taste of being responsible for the oversight of multiple outlets. I had to order all of the product for our a la carte clubhouse lunch and dinner menus. I also needed to keep up with all of the catered events such as golf tournaments, weddings, birthday parties, Sunday Brunch, and so forth. There was also product for the beverage carts out on the course. Next, I had to plan the logistics behind putting out food for catered events while maintaining proper service to the dining room.

One of the things I used to absolutely dread was the boxed lunch. Now it sounds like it should have been the easiest of all the meals. Not so. Again, culinary-wise it was a snap. It did require however, many steps, perfect timing and a lot of space. Let's say we had a medium size tournament of seventy-five people. The lunch would include usually a sandwich consisting of ham or turkey, lettuce, tomato and a mayo and mustard packet. There would also be an individually wrapped cookie and a bag of chips. First I would have to slice enough ham and/or turkey for seventy-five sandwiches while slicing enough tomatoes and separating and cleaning the leaf lettuce. I also sliced the cheese, covered it and stored it in the cooler. Then I would lay out the hoagie rolls on the stainless steel prep tables. This was tricky because you can't do too many at once or else the bread would start to get stale by the time you finished processing them. I cut open all of the bread rolls and started filling them with meat, lettuce, tomato and cheese. Once one batch was finished I quickly wrapped them individually in plastic wrap and placed them in the walk-in cooler, then on to the next batch until they were all completed.

Next, the cookies had to be baked. I will admit we used pre-made dough, which was just fine with me given our tight staffing and equipment constraints. After cooling, the cookies were individually wrapped and set aside. This all had to be done the evening before, because tournaments were usually scheduled for early morning start times. Meanwhile, dinner service was going on and I had to be available to help my lone line cook should he get in the weeds. I also had to be careful not to get in his way as he was wheeling and dealing.

At the end of the night when service was over, I was free to finish the lunches. I had to unfold all of the empty lunch boxes and set them up on the prep table. This was where I was free to put as many out as could possibly fit. To make keeping track of the count easier, I usually put out all of them at one time which meant utilizing every inch of counter space available. Next was assembly time: One cookie, mayo and mustard packet, one bag of chips and one napkin. These semi-full boxes would stay "as is" until the next morning at which time I would finish them with the sandwiches from the cooler. After the addition of the cold sandwiches that morning we closed the boxes and the servers picked them up prior to tee time. The process doesn't sound very involved but it proved to be quite tedious every time.

If we were in Japan, these "on the go" meals would be served in what are called bento boxes. These are staples in Japanese dining, and range from hand-made lacquer stackables to foam disposables. Through the course of time, they became more and more refined. During the Edo Dynasty in Japan, the Makuno-uchi bento (*between acts*-bento) came into fashion. This was an elegant boxed meal served between acts at Kabuki theater performances. We can say that the golfers at Bloomingdale Golfer's Club were enjoying their Mackuno-uchi bentos between the front nine and the back nine out on the course. Bentos can be *soigne* with a very articulate, organized appearance. Similarly, my first shot at the helm was forcing me to learn how to run a clean and organized operation.

One habit I remember picking up from Chef Dieter back at Weston Hills was what I'll call the "clipboard method." I found seven clipboards and labeled each one with a day of the week. They were hung on a wall just inside the entrance to the kitchen. Each time I was given a copy of the contract sheet for an event I reviewed it then put it on the corresponding clipboard. If it was more than a week away it went behind any event on the board for an earlier week. So if there was an event for Tuesday of next week, it would go on the Tuesday clipboard behind this Tuesday's event.

This simple practice is an absolute *must* in a multi-outlet operation. It not only kept me organized, it allowed everyone from the cooks, to the servers, and anyone else interested, to know exactly what was coming up. Even members of the marketing department could come by and make sure I had the correct information for each event. I was always checking and rechecking those sheets to make sure I had all of my ordering done.

To add another twist to the whole thing, I could only receive deliveries on certain days. Our purveyor had us set on a specific two-days-a-week delivery schedule. I had to pay really close attention to what product was needed for each event, while remembering to order everything for our a la carte lunch and dinner menus. There were also the beverage carts that couldn't be forgotten about.

Doing a monthly inventory count was also an absolute must. The Food and Beverage Director (Kevin) and I counted all of the food product in the entire facility. We also counted all of the alcoholic and non-alcoholic beverages; every bottle of liquor, every bottle of beer, every bottled water, Gatorade, soda, etc. As if we didn't typically work late enough, those "end of the month" nights carried with them some *seriously* late hours. I had actually gotten a taste of monthly inventory a few years earlier while working for Macaroni Grill.

I remember one year during my stent as Sous chef there, the last day of November fell on a Thursday. Yes, Thanksgiving Thursday to be exact. All of us managers had to stay and count inventory after working all day. 'Twas in deed the life we had chosen, as ugly as it seemed at times. As a matter of fact, the New Year's Eve in 1999 ended up being the only one I would have off during my entire culinary career. With this position, also came flooding back to me that notion of being trapped behind the eight ball. After that short two-month stent at *Norman's*, that elusive thing known as job satisfaction was once again hiding behind the eight ball. The hunt was on yet again. For this reason, I was already searching for the next thing pretty much from the moment I landed the position at Bloomingdale. I had started there in January of 2000 and by the beginning of June had already found another job.

In late May of 2000 I started my Executive Chef position at Walden Lakes Country Club. It's nestled within a gated community in Plant City, which is just east of Valrico. This was a larger facility with two golf courses, a down stairs dining room for members only, and two upstairs banquet rooms. There was a full kitchen in the a la carte dining room down stairs, and a large banquet kitchen upstairs.

Though the operation was much bigger, my staff wasn't much bigger. There were two full-time restaurant cooks and two full-time banquet cooks. We had one full-time dishwasher and one guy that did double duty between dish pit and banquet cook. Then there was me, and above me was our Food and Beverage Director. She had been very involved with banquet prep and product ordering before I came on board. She was one of the hardest working people I have met, even to this day. One of my first goals was to get things going, so she could be freed-up to focus on the other duties involved in running the Food and Beverage Department. We made a very good team. As she received positive feed-back from the members, she felt more confident to let go of the reigns a little more and I was off and running.

Our restaurant was only open for lunch during the week, but we served dinner every Friday night and Saturday night. We hosted a lot of wedding receptions on Saturday nights in the banquet department as well. The facility also hosted many golf tournaments since we had two golf courses. This allowed for a tournament to be planned for one course, while other golfers could still enjoy our second course. Additionally, we held Family Night in the restaurant on the last Friday of every month which was by reservation only.

Above all of my other tasks, I enjoyed the Family Night dinners the most because I created a special limited menu each time. It was my break from the norm while also allowing me to flex some culinary muscle. The most important thing I learned about it though, was how to successfully introduce patrons to who you are as a culinary professional. It's not enough to have fancy sounding food if people don't know what it is and don't want to eat it.

The Walden Lakes community was built right in the middle of Plant City, which is largely a farming town. The main crop is strawberries. Every year in March, everyone in the Tampa Bay area attends a two-week harvest celebration called the Plant City Strawberry Festival. It's basically their version of the Florida State Fair held in Tampa every February. It includes games, bumper cars, exhibits, concerts and even a midway with rides. I actually enjoy it more than the Florida State Fair, which has gotten a little off the chain with our rambunctious youth at times. You can buy anything strawberry, from a half-flat or full flat of fresh strawberries, to live strawberry plants, to ridiculously good strawberry shortcake.

Our facility was once asked to contribute a pan of food to a local event. Being in the capital of Florida strawberry harvesting, I decided to make a pan of strawberry-peppercorn glazed pork loin. The goal was to utilize something everyone loved (strawberries) in an unfamiliar way. I can't recall everything I put in the glaze, but it came out very nicely and they gave us good feedback. In creating each Family Night menu, I found a balance between utilizing familiar raw ingredients and introducing new techniques. I quickly realized there was no sense in trying to give them something ripped from the pages of the *Norman's* menu. These were good, hard working folks who wanted an elegant meal that they would understand and enjoy. I was learning how to make good food that was also relevant. It actually worked, and I developed a small following of devotees during those meals. It was a good lesson in finding my own voice versus just regurgitating someone else's words.

As busy as my career had been thus far, things on the home front were about to get even busier. Just a few weeks after starting at Walden Lakes, I was in the banquet kitchen one day doing some prep work. It was June 14 to be exact. The kitchen phone rang (I still didn't have a cell phone) and I answered it. It happened to be my mother-in-law. I remember exactly how the conversation went. I said, "Hey mama, what's up?" She replied, "You, you're up. It's time!" My heart leapt. She had taken Lisa to her doctor's appointment that morning and he decided to send her to the hospital, which was right across the street from his office. It was time to deliver a baby! Man it was about to be on and popping. I let my boss know the situation and headed out the door. We had a plan already in place and Lisa had previously given me strict instructions for this very moment.

I raced home, grabbed her packed suitcase, and drove to the hospital. I was all over it. I was so on it that I brought the whole suitcase right into the delivery room. I'm sure I looked like a complete nut. Lisa was like, "Dude, it's for after the delivery when I get assigned to my room. You could have left that thing in the car. Just put it in the bathroom for now." Her mom and the nurse looked at me like, "Wow…yeah…okay." I checked out the scene and all seemed well. To be honest, this is where our testimony differs from so many people I've talked to. The whole labor and delivery experience for us was very peaceful and calm. We had attended a four-week class on Thursdays that was held at the hospital and it prepared us for the labor and delivery process. It also covered newborn care once we got home. We implemented the breathing techniques we had chosen to use during the class. Her mom was in the room redirecting her during the moments when she got a little excited. It was a very divine experience. There was no cursing, no slapping, no evil eye. There was no yelling of any kind.

She started pushing at about 8pm, and at 9:09pm Chloe Narrice made her debut into the world. Now, I do understand that it was two hundred times easier for me than for Lisa but it did go very smoothly. I attribute it to the fact that she had read a book called *Supernatural Child Birth* by Jackie Mize. Lisa devoted herself to the affirmations contained in its pages. I'm not saying that if someone doesn't have a delivery experience like ours. that it's because they didn't pray. I don't believe in making someone feel like they didn't have enough faith or did something wrong when things don't go the way they would have liked. Life is full of difficulties, whether we pray or not. I do think in our case God honored our dedication to the process.

Unfortunately, I don't remember much of the first year of Chloe's life, because I was busy with work. While Lisa was at home taking care of her, I worked some serious hours. We were insanely busy between wedding rehearsal dinners, wedding receptions, golf tournaments, business meetings, weekly Rotary Club meetings, a la carte dining, Family Night dinners, monthly inventory, and manager's meetings.

Karen (my boss) and her husband Bob also ran a dinner theater out of the facility. He would write the scripts, choreograph the dances and manage the actors as they not only rehearsed and performed but also set-up and broke down their own stage and props. They also waited on the tables before hitting the stage to entertain the clients. The music was provided by a live band of which Bob was the leader and drummer. Karen had the kitchen staff and me to handle all of the food. During busy season I would work between sixty and seventy hours per week. God is good, and there eventually came an opportunity to spend quality time with Chloe. Each Monday, we had our manager's meeting, so I took every Tuesday off. After the first year, Lisa went back to work and Chloe went to the daycare on the property. I kept her home on Tuesdays and we spent the entire day together.

Still being consumed with improving my skills, there were many times during slow season when I would be up all night researching things on the computer and creating menu ideas. I also began studying the works of another star chef. I was first introduced to his food philosophy while working at *Norman's*. We would get carbon copies of articles written about different chefs making waves on the national scene. Now I was reading everything I could about Thomas Keller who owns The French Laundry in Yountville, California in the Napa Valley. Just reading that first article about him made me sit up and take notice. The way he spoke about food and technique completely intimidated me. Before long, Lisa bought me his book simply titled *The French Laundry Cookbook*. Some of the lessons in it seemed more like mad science rather than cooking. The most memorable concept I learned from it was chlorophyll extraction. Yes, in his restaurant they actually extract and use the chlorophyll from leafy greens. They add it to things like pasta dough and sauces. One day when I was off from the country club I decided to give it a shot. In the recipe he used spinach, parsley and watercress. I went with a much cheaper head of iceberg lettuce. To my complete satisfaction it actually worked. After a two-day process, I was looking at about a tablespoon's worth of green pigment which resembled paint. I was completely stoked. It was ultra-light, airy, and tasted like the essence of lettuce. Of course, as I dug further into studying cuisine I *wasn't* cooking, that eight ball was again blocking my view.

Soon the usual ills of working for a corporately owned facility started to wear on my nerves. As with every other company I worked for, my patience had worn thin for dealing with things not being the way I believed they should be. Karen and Bob had since moved to another city where she was the Food and Beverage Director of a thirty-six-hole facility. With three golf courses they were most assuredly very busy. I'm sure she did well, because she put her heart into everything she did.

After some searching I found out that the Holiday Inn in Downtown Tampa was looking for an Executive Chef. It was a three hundred room hotel which was located directly across the street from The Tampa Performing Arts Center (now the David A. Straz Center). I got an initial interview with the General Manager, and then he called me back for a second one. Prior to the second interview he did some investigating into my previous employment. He told me about a friend of his who was a member at Walden Lakes Country Club. He added that the friend was very impressed with my cooking, having been in attendance at a small dinner I did for the Advisory board at the club. It was a five course meal by invitation only, and it was held in one of the ball rooms. Only about twenty people were there, which included the club general manager and my boss. The general manager at the Holiday Inn said it was one of the best meals his friend had ever eaten, and with that, he offered me the job.

I was of course, nervous and very excited. At Walden Lakes I was making $34,000 per year, and now I would be making $37,500 a year. That was the highest salary I had ever made in my entire life, and remember, I was still a high school dropout. That excitement was, however, severely tempered by nervousness. This time it was because during my tour of the property prior to accepting the position I saw things I didn't like. There was old, outdated equipment which hadn't been properly maintained. The kitchen brigade was small although, I did at least have a banquet chef to assist with all of the catering. I could feel I was taking a job that wouldn't satisfy me, but with a toddler at home we needed more income. If *Norman's* was a ten on the sleepless nights stress-o-meter, then Holiday Inn would prove to be a thirty on a ten point scale.

I started the new job in early 2002, and soon after we found out we were pregnant again! We decided that Lisa would stay home and tend to the home front, while pregnant with a toddler running around. My increase in income had come just in time.

Unfortunately, this job did prove to be an absolute back breaker for several reasons. First of all, I quickly came to learn that the hotel was having financial problems. There were certain vendors I couldn't order from because we owed them too much money. My boss (the Food and Beverage Director) was like the Artful Dodger. When confronted by a vendor, he always came up with creative reasons for lack of payment. Other times he would tell the person, "I'll be right back," and disappear for about an hour. The hotel was franchised by a family that was not very involved with the staff. When they walked through the kitchen they never spoke to anyone.

Another reason this job was a back breaker was because of the crazy schedule. Man, I thought I worked some long hours in the past; this job took workaholic to a new level. We had one breakfast cook, one lunch cook and two dinner cooks. The breakfast cook worked six days a week so I only had to cover one day for him. On that day I would come in at 5:30am to set-up and work breakfast. Then when my lunch cook came in I would make sure he was good to go then check-in with the banquet chef. She was awesome. Her husband worked the dish pit and when I say she looked out for her man, I mean she looked out for her man. She made sure he took his breaks and that he ate a good meal every shift. I made sure everything was on schedule with her then I checked over all of my ordering for the upcoming banquets.

We stayed pretty busy because the hotel sat a few blocks from the Hillsborough River where the University of Tampa rowing team practiced. We hosted visiting rowing teams that would be in town to have a couple of weeks of practice before competing against UT. Every morning the athletes would come downstairs and have a special breakfast buffet then after practice, we had a lunch buffet ready for them.

This was in addition to the other hotel guests. As we moved into the evening, we would have guests from the outside coming into the restaurant to enjoy a pre-show meal, before heading across the street to the Performing Arts Center. We also had whatever banquets to prepare and serve that evening. On many of these days when I started the morning at 5:30am as the breakfast cook, I wouldn't go home until about 11:00pm that night. On a normal day though, I worked from about 8:30am until between 11:00pm and 1:00am. I worked six days a week and even on my day off I was constantly plotting and planning. My mood was always fluctuating. One moment I would be smiling and the next I would be ready to snap a neck. I had a very benevolent way of managing people, so I carried a lot of the stress home with me rather than yell at the staff. They were good people who, like me, happened to work for people that were not very good employers. There was no reason to take my frustrations with the company out on them. God had always made me very conscious of how I treat my employees. The stress was nonetheless taking a toll on me.

I remember my boss sitting me down in his office one day and asking me an odd question. He said, "Has anyone ever told you that you were manic depressive?" I was like, "Excuse me?!" He continued, "You just seem to always have drastic mood swings." I replied, "No, nobody has ever said that to me." I sat for a moment thinking to myself, "No, it's you fools that are making me crazy!" He went on to suggest that I take a Saturday and Sunday off and go away with the family for a weekend of relaxation. I actually took him up on that offer. Boy was I sorry! We had gone to the east coast of Florida and checked into a hotel near the beach. I ended up being on the phone with my boss several times working out the product ordering for each event and putting out fires from a couple hundred miles away. I didn't relax at all the entire weekend. Even though I wasn't physically working, my nerves were being worked over-time. That was the last weekend I took off while working that job.

A third reason this job was an intense back breaker was because of the stability, or lack thereof. Apparently, the hotel was in worse financial trouble than I thought. About four months after I started working there, the Holiday Inn Corporation moved an office into the building. The franchise family was under close scrutiny. I found out they were in danger of losing the license to bear the Holiday Inn name. Soon the pendulum started swinging. Every week the human resources director would walk a member of the executive management team into her office. When the person emerged he or she was officially unemployed. The HR Director became this feared individual. Nobody liked seeing her coming. She was the Summoner doing the company's bidding. I watched as the Director of Housekeeping went, the Parking Services Director went, so on and so forth. That pendulum was silently swinging back and forth, each pass claiming another victim. Everyday all of us managers were wondering, "Is it going to be me today?" It was a very stressful way to have to work.

There was yet a fourth reason why I considered this job an absolute back breaker. I faced something I had never faced before...mutiny. There were two cooks actually plotting to take over the kitchen...seriously. Lord have mercy, I had seen it all! My boss had hired a new cook who came in with some good experience. He immediately connected with another cook that I had hired not too long before. I first started noticing that the cook I hired began just doing his own thing with some of the lunch buffet items that were not kosher with me, yet he continued to do it anyway. Then I noticed the cook my boss had hired was always trying to "encourage" me to look for other opportunities of employment.

He also spent a lot of time in my boss's office. He even went so far as to set me up with the owner of a local pub just down the street. Believe it or not I went and interviewed for the position. This is where I was truly leaning on God. I didn't want to limit God and figured it might be a blessing in disguise. Sometimes it takes extreme discomfort to move us into our destiny. Maybe it wasn't a conspiracy between these two cooks. Maybe it was part of a master plan organized by my boss himself who didn't have a reason to outright fire me. I was walking very circumspectly through the entire situation. As my high school football coaches used to say, I was keeping my head on a swivel. Paying attention to my surroundings and considering all possibilities.

That pub job turned out not to be anything I was interested in. I didn't have to worry about this attempted "coup" for very long though because that silent pendulum soon swung my way. I had already rehearsed my approach in the event my number should come up. When the H.R. Director sat me down I requested a letter on company letterhead that said I was being laid off due to company cuts and not due to poor job performance. She obliged and about a week and a half later when I went to pick-up my last check she had the letter ready. By the time I had gone back to get it the General Manager had been let go. I later heard that the HR director herself was fired. I felt so bad for her because we all knew she was going to eventually get her walking papers. It's just such a terrible position to put a person in by making her fire all of us managers knowing she was going to be the final casualty in the end. A few months later, while driving past downtown one day, I noticed that the hotel no longer displayed the Holiday Inn logo. That pendulum had swung in a complete circle and finally reached the hand that originally set it in motion.

From the short time I spent at the Holiday Inn, I have one vivid culinary memory. There was a server in the restaurant who was married to a Jamaican, and she loved cooking Jamaican food. One day she was telling me about boiled bananas. They were one of her favorite things to make and she agreed to make us some when time permitted. As a chef, I'm always willing to try new things. It's like a disease, chefs just can't resist trying something we've never had before.

So she made these boiled bananas one day and all of the kitchen and front of the house staff tried them. I have to say I absolutely hated them! Now, I love Jamaican food but I didn't like anything about those darn boiled bananas. Maybe she made them wrong. I'm not sure. All I know is, I couldn't stand anything about them. I sheepishly ate them and just nodded my head and walked away. I don't like being rude when it comes to someone sharing with me something dear to them. But I really did not like those bad boys. I found no redeeming quality about them.

This memory reminds me that sometimes we have experiences in which there seems to be no good aspect about the situation. The Holiday Inn was that moment in my culinary career. In just six months, I had been worked half to death, labeled manic depressive, plotted against, and fed something I found completely unpalatable. It was what it was. At the time, that period of my career seemed to have no redeeming quality other than being a season meant to endure.

Amid this entire experience, one very poignant moment stands out. I still remember as clear as day, when I pulled into the parking space in front of our apartment and prepared myself. I had to tell Lisa that even though she was relying on me to take care of her, Chloe, and the one on the way, I now had no job to support us. As I parked and turned the car off I sat in silence with my eyes welling up with tears. I had endured all manner of insults to my ego, but the thing that finally broke me was the thought of not being the hero. It was now time to be a man.

Alas, there was yet a redeeming quality to this season after all. It was drawing me closer to God. The entire time that pendulum was swinging I hadn't asked God to save my job. Instead, I had been praying that His will be done. I was growing tired of working a million hours a week just to keep a job that didn't supply all of my needs according to His riches in glory. Subtly I was beginning to rely on Him and I didn't even realize it.

Being that God is forever faithful, I landed another job after a couple of weeks. One of my purveyors at the Holiday Inn knew a friend of the Executive Chef at Bern's Steak House and he put in a good word for me. During my interview with the chef, we discussed my travels in South Florida. Until this point, I had been putting my two-month apprenticeship at Norman's on my resume. But nobody in Tampa knew of him except for the folks at Mise En Place Catering. While the chef and I were talking I mentioned Chef Norman and she was like, "Why didn't you put that on your resume?" I was honest and said, "Because nobody in Tampa so far seems to know who he is so I left it off this time." She then told me that he was her idol. Go figure! The one time I left his name off of my resume was the one time it had relevance. It was another lesson.

Don't ever give up, keep doing what you're doing and it will eventually pay off.

Well, I got the job and she took an immediate liking to me. Once again God had shown me favor. I started right around July 4, 2002 and on July 20, 2002 Lauryn Antoinette made her big entrance into the world. We were now the Edwards four. Our family was growing and we were very excited but that belt was tightening up really quickly.

Bern's Steak House is an iconic establishment in the SoHo (South Howard) district of South Tampa. It was started by Bern Laxer in 1956, but by the time I started there his son David Laxer had taken over operations. I have to say he was one of the best employers I have ever worked for. He was the complete opposite of the owners at my previous job; a very sharp business man, yet a very approachable person. Bern's was an extremely unique experience.

The best way I've been able to describe it to people is to say that in a perfect world Bern's could serve as a hospitality school. You could work your way around the huge kitchen, learning every station including the dessert room which has it's own separate culinary operation. It would be an extensive journey, as you travel through the fish station with it's six hundred-gallon tank stocked with live fish. Then maybe visit the sauté station, with its large woks over open burners at one end, and fast paced action on the range burners at the other end. Next, you may work the meat cutting station, where each steak is actually cut to order. Of course that would have to be followed by the grill station, where the fresh-cut steaks are seared on a custom thirty two square foot grill. Next, your tour of duty may take you through the salad, potato, and soup stations; all of which having their own sphere of influence. It really is an extensive operation.

You would also make your way upstairs into the sweet life, to work in the dessert kitchen of the Harry Waugh (Wah) Room. After touring and learning each station in the kitchen you could easily get a job anywhere and feel right at home. Your journey wouldn't stop there though. It just so happens that Bern's has the largest private wine collection in the world. You would most definitely have to do a stent as a wine steward, unlocking the history of many bottles untold. They have a wine shop which also offers classes to the public. I got a chance to attend a couple of them while working there. Let's not forget the farm. Bern's maintains it's own farm that raises organic produce specifically for the restaurant.

Beyond all of this, should you feel especially adventurous, you could make the two-year commitment to becoming a waiter. Bern's takes guest service very, very seriously. In order to become a dining room server you must first become a "red coat." These are the back waiters, who learn how to coordinate all of the food orders for each table from the kitchen and run each tray into the dining room. They set it up on a tray stand and the front waiter (black coat) does the honors of serving it to the guests. The black coats are seasoned veterans, who are tasked with meeting the guest's every need before, during, and after the food is served. They are well versed in wines to help make suitable selections to accompany the meal. Their job is to stay with the table through the entire dining experience while the red coats hustle for any incidentals that are requested. It is a grueling two-year process to trade that red coat in for a black coat. However, once they don the black coat, it is like being inducted into a society of achievers.

This intricate exploration of Bern's operations would, of course be in a perfect world. In actual practice, the restaurant is far too busy to allow an individual the liberty to smoothly move from one area to the next. Typically, as in any busy establishment, you get in where you fit in, and learn all you can until another spot comes open. My spot from the get-go was the grill station. Here is why I chose filet of beef for the protein in the title of this chapter. I cooked more cuts of beef at Bern's than in all my other jobs combined. Bern's is primarily known for three things; great service, great wines and great steaks. We even had a walk-in cooler specifically for aging certain cuts of meat. Everything about the steaks exuded impeccable quality. Our custom grill was even fueled by natural petrified wood charcoal.

I started at Bern's just before my twenty-ninth birthday, and that clock was ticking louder than ever. This was my first non-management job in a few years and, though not having the responsibility was comforting, the notion of not making progress was burning a hole in me. We had a very hard-pressing executive chef and she seemed to never let up. At one point, we had a heated conversation and she voiced the opinion that I was just relaxing and enjoying the reduced responsibilities of the current position. She was really looking for me to take over the grill station and become the leader. She called me out on my ego in front of the rest of the staff. It was very humbling, especially considering the fact that she seemed very narcissistic herself.

I remember God dealing with me immediately on that issue. I seemed to only want to receive certain messages from certain people. The problem was that it became more about the messenger, and less about the one who sent the message. God sometimes chooses the unlikely thing to send a clear message, and it can be missed if we pay more attention to the mode of transport, and less attention to the actual message. That was a very jagged pill to swallow.

We had another heated discussion about my expectations. She said that I had these unrealistic ideas in my mind about how things should be and couldn't relate to how life actually happens, which was another big wake-up call. I hadn't realized until that point I was so harshly judging everything around me, that there was no way for me to relate to anything or anyone. In my mind everything was "out of whack." Nothing measured up to the perfect vision I had of how it ought to be. She was right, but I couldn't acknowledge it at the time.

I had reached a place of realizing that the values my parents drummed into me, were not always the same values the rest of the world had. They taught me to work hard and to be honest. I was finding that there were many people seeming to succeed with very sloppy work performance and not much honesty. This discrepancy was causing me major stress. The dream of working hard and getting ahead was slowly dying within me.

With hope fading, pessimism was setting in fast. It was apparent to me that in many cases real life was more about *who* you know, and not so much about *what* you know. Being the best at what I did meant less to my bosses than being someone they felt comfortable around and could get along with. I was becoming awakened to the realities of the world's system, and it was causing me to be more and more isolated at work and in life in general. I was increasingly unhappy with everything. With all of the stern teaching I got from my parents, I didn't learn how to navigate life when it doesn't line-up with your expectations.

Proverbs 4:7 says, "Wisdom is the principal thing; therefore get wisdom: but with all your getting get understanding." I had always sought wisdom, but God was in the midst of teaching me understanding. It was definitely less about what I knew and more about who I knew. I've seen it written, "No Jesus, no peace. Know Jesus, know peace." But I still wasn't seeking to know Him better. As a result, the learning process was becoming very, very painful.

My fall back was to become as busy as possible in an attempt to provide for the family. I briefly took on a part-time job at Eighth Avenue Grill in the Ybor (ee-bore) City district of Tampa.

I worked the lunch shift for a few months, then I gave it up for a prep position at Bern's. So I would work the morning prep shift at Bern's, break for lunch, and then come back for the dinner shift on the grill. All of this working of course wasn't enough, as Lisa and I found out we were pregnant with child number three. We made the decision to move to a cheaper place. This time we were going to be back in the hood. It was the only affordable place we could find, so we packed everything and moved to an apartment on 22nd Street just north of Fletcher Avenue. This was in the middle of the University Area, which is also part of that infamous "suitcase city" I hailed from about ten years earlier. I was back on my old stomping grounds.

On December 6, 2003 Nyomi Michelle made her triumphant entrance into the world, and we were now the Edwards Five. Lisa and I were so proud of our growing family, and we wanted to give our daughters every opportunity we could to succeed in life. We eventually started going back to church. After a brief time at a mega-church, we settled on a very small non-denominational place where we felt right at home from the beginning.

Through the course of time, our pastor started making home visits with all of the members. I remember he had come to visit us just as we were planning our move to suitcase city. I was frustrated and said to him, "It just seems like since we came back to Tampa we have been steadily going backwards." What I didn't realize was that the Lord was drawing us closer and closer to Him the entire time.

It was interesting because even though our family was getting bigger, we were moving into a smaller place. A large part of this was because we were fervent in our commitment to having Lisa stay home with the girls until they all were in school. Income would be very tight for a lot of years to come. When Nyomi was still a baby we had the old crib from both of her sisters. One side was broken so I removed it and pushed the crib against the wall so the missing side was facing the wall. All three girls shared one room and Lisa and I had the other room. It was quaint but we made it work. We also got more involved in church, but my inner restlessness continued to take a toll on our relationship. I continued to have periodic episodes of staying out all night. I was unhappy with everything all the time. Professionally I was at wit's end. I began looking for another job, once again.

Around July 4, 2003, just about a year to the day after starting at Bern's, I started working at Carrabba's Italian Grill. Even though I had managerial experience, they didn't hire managers from the outside, so I was offered a grill cook position. From the beginning, the humbling process continued where it left off at Bern's. As with Jonah and the whale, it is impossible to run from God. For if we understand that he is everywhere, then we also understand that to run *from* Him is to run straight *into* Him. It was my first experience with workplace bullying. Between our general manager and the lead cook on the line, I used to hate going to work each evening. I can remember sitting in my car in the parking lot before some shifts and praying, because I absolutely dreaded the thought of going inside. The singular reason I stuck with it that first year was because my family was counting on me. Man, was it tough though. I don't think I had ever wanted to fight anyone so badly as I wanted to mix it up with that lead cook.

He was one of the best in the company at running the line, and for that reason he had the GM in his hip pocket. I despised everything about them. To me they resembled two thugs going to and fro seeking to strike fear and trepidation in the hearts of the rest of the staff. The GM consistently turned in great numbers, so the company loved him. It was clear the two of them weren't going anywhere anytime soon. The grill station dictated the pace of the rest of the line because it took the longest for things to cook. So the lead cook's trick to keeping his ticket times low was to call for food from the grill sooner than it would normally be ready. He would be standing a few feet away from me barking out requests to sell items that just went on the grill a few minutes earlier. He would yell down to the other stations to sell the food for that table and of course, the grilled meat better be on the plate when everything else is going out. The GM always worked as the expeditor, so if I was trailing anything, you can bet he would start yelling for whatever was missing. There was a triangle of tension between the three of us that I don't think anyone wanted to get in the middle of.

I guess it takes a hard head to know a hard head, because in time I actually started getting along with both of them. During this time I got even more involved in church. Slowly my attitude started softening towards them as I began to finally take hold of the lessons started back at Bern's. I was beginning to learn how to relate to others through humility. That, combined with my hard work ethic, caused both of them to respect me more as well. It's interesting how that worked. I *got* more respect when I decided to *give* more respect. During 2003 I also went back and got my GED. I was finally a high school graduate...equivalent!

Though Lisa and I continued to go through our relationship difficulties, we were managing to get more serious with church. Eventually, I went through a year-long grooming and was ordained as a deacon, along with two other gentlemen. Lisa became one of the women's leaders and the hospitality director. We also were able to buy our first home. It was on the opposite end of 22nd Street further south in an area we call Central Tampa. It was however, still in the hood. We were just happy to finally have something to call our own. After being at Carrabba's for about two years, I began praying for the Lord to send me a job where what I did for a living would bless people. I understood that for the most part, everyone we fed in the restaurant was pretty well off. I wanted to make a difference in people's lives. While volunteering in various capacities through our church outreaches, I really felt a deep compassion for those in need.

Being that old habits die hard, I once again decided to fill my extra time with another job. I worked at Carrabba's during the evenings, so I found a job working the lunch shift at Mise En Place Restaurant of all places. After a waiting period of about four years, I finally got hired. The cool thing is that I worked the sauté station, which was right next to Chef Marty Blitz's work station. He didn't work the line per se, but he prepped a lot of sauces for dinner and other special project items while we worked the lunch crowd. If someone needed help he would jump in. I was literally rubbing elbows with another pioneer in Florida cuisine.

Mise En Place is a three-star establishment that has been very instrumental in shaping Tampa's food scene. Chef Marty was a very down-to-earth type of guy. He demanded excellence, but he also was a bit of a jokester. I really enjoyed working for him. This three-star, highly acclaimed restaurant was the first and only place where I got to make collard greens *my way* and serve them to the patrons. I love some heat in my greens so they came out spicy, but everyone liked them.

I was also responsible for a dish called Tajine. It's a North African dish cooked in a special pot of the same name. The bottom is flat and round while the top is funnel-shaped to allow for the natural moisture to evaporate from the food product, condense on the inside of the lid and then run back down the sloping sides of it's funnel shape. It creates a sauce without having to add much water which works well in parts of Africa where water is scarce. We didn't have a tajine to prepare it in, but the sauce was very tasty nonetheless. For me the inclusion of dishes like these, marks a shift in haute cuisine in America that I am very pleased to see has occurred. Within the past two decades, it has become more fashionable to showcase ethnic foods and methods of preparation. New American cuisine is really about bringing all of the food stuffs and traditions from the native lands of our forefathers and applying both classical and innovative techniques of preparation. What has resulted, in my opinion, is a very diverse and conscious style of high-quality restaurant food and service. I'm pleased to see that high-end restaurants are serving food that more resembles who we are as a nation; diverse yet unified. I think the capstone to this movement would be to have Native American ingredients and techniques figure more prominently on menus by non-Native American chefs.

As I drew closer to God I became busier with Kingdom endeavors, and had less patience for working those fifty million hour weeks anymore. After about a year, I left my part-time position at Mise En Place. Now my mornings were free, and after some time, I started leading the nursing home outreach our pastor and associate pastor had been taking turns leading. Eventually, the nursing home offered me a job as an activities assistant. I would be working in their pediatric unit with the special needs children. It seemed my prayers had been answered. I was finally going to be helping people with my work. Oh but wait, there was just one catch; one huge catch. It was a four-dollar-an-hour cut in pay, as if things weren't tight enough already.

So now in order to finally step into doing something for a living that helped people in need, I was going to have to step out in some serious faith. Lisa was going to have to take that trip along with me. Whewww, talk about pressure. I thought about it, spoke to Lisa and then spoke to our pastor. Finally I made a decision.

After a four-year stint at Carrabba's, I turned in my two-week notice. I was trading in my chef whites for medical scrubs. At the age of thirty-two my culinary career was over. I had cooked my last steak, sautéed my last pasta, and I was closing the doors on that phase of my life. It was all I had done since I was sixteen years old, with the exception of a few odd jobs here and there. What would this next phase be like? I wasn't sure, but I was eager to find out.

"*Sometimes life is like molten chocolate: hot with bitter aggression yet sweet with refined richness.*"

~NME

Chapter 8:

˜MOLTEN CHOCOLATE CAKE˜

Now came the sweet life. I was working in an environment that was ten times less hostile than what I was used to. I found there to be much less aggression and way, way more control of the tongue. As an interesting side note; there seemed to be a lot more Christians working in health care than in hospitality. Why, I don't know. I'm not sure if it's a spiritual thing, or if some other factors are at play.

The nursing home had three separate buildings on its campus. We expanded the outreach and so my wife, the girls, and I were leading services in each building. In time, I transferred from the activities department to work in the rehab department. Now I was working as a rehab tech and learning a boat load of stuff. This was, however, tempered by the unfortunate reality that I simply wasn't making enough money, and we ended up losing our home to foreclosure.

We once again moved in with Lisa's parents and continued to press on. Soon, I enrolled in school to become a Physical

Therapist Assistant. At the tender age of thirty-five I was a college freshman. It was an accelerated associate degree program, which took me twenty-three months to complete. It was very rigorous, and at times I felt like I wasn't going to make it. The professors advised us students not to work while moving through the program. For me that wasn't an option. I had a family to support.

It was probably the most difficult two years of my life, besides these last two years. I attended classes during the day and worked in the evening. After work I helped the girls with their homework, and finally, did my homework until the late-night hours. I worked Saturdays to help make-up hours I missed during the week. It was hard but God provided and I graduated Cum Laude with a 3.66 overall GPA.

While in school, I had stepped down from my Deacon position at church because I couldn't properly fulfill my duties. There was no time for things like watching TV, let alone helping serve the flock. I will humbly admit that I was also looking for a way out. I was starting to feel stretched at all ends and wanted to be a little selfish with my time. We started attending church less, and eventually stopped going all together. After graduating, I went to work at two different facilities trying to make some cash. About two years later, Lisa enrolled in the same program at the same university. Another two years after that, and we were both PTAs.

Enter the molten chocolate cake. It's a style of cake that's partially baked, a lump of chocolate is pressed into the center, then it continues baking until it resembles a moist, chocolate cake. The kicker is that once you cut it open with the side of a fork, this bubbling hot "molten lava" comes flowing out. Lisa and I were in a position in which one would think we were now on our way. We had both finally earned college degrees and were making good money. Instead, this is when the bottom fell out. We presented as this beautifully baked confection but it took just the right amount of pressure and everything under the surface came flowing out.

One night, I stayed out all night, and that was it. I ended up sleeping in my car for ten days, while continuing to work and save to get an apartment. We remained separated for about a year and four months, and then on September 10, 2015 the judge banged down the gavel and we were divorced. It was over. Twenty years, nine months and nine days had come and gone. We began this journey at twenty-one and nineteen years of age and at forty-two and thirty-nine, we had called it quits. We were both exhausted. I think earning our college degrees pushed us closer to the point of being willing to let go. Maybe each felt the other could survive now, being able to earn a decent income. That, combined with not diligently seeking the Lord, catapulted us toward the inevitable. Neither of us had anything left to give.

I have since been flooded with an onslaught of emotions. One of which is embarrassment. I have been feeling like this is a blight on my Christian record, if you will. The absolute shame of knowing you were unsuccessful at wife husbandry after toiling with it for twenty years. It is probably the only thing I have endeavored to do, that no matter how hard I tried, I wasn't able to succeed. I really was not a good husband.

Being alone in my apartment, with nothing to keep me company but my thoughts, was maddening at times. I still was too stubborn to seek God, but I did become more introspective. My poetry soon took the form of a man tormented. One night I was driving home after hanging out, and I was suddenly hit with this overwhelming sorrow. For some reason, it felt like I had driven those same streets for the last twenty years and gotten nowhere. When I got home, I sat down with pencil and paper and began writing.

The Home Town
So sad is the hometown from whence we have come,
You feel safety in staying, I feel a yearning to leave.
I remember walking these streets in the blistering summer sun,
Shoes with holes in them, a borrowed shirt and shorts.
I also remember huddling behind the convenient store,
Surviving the chilling winter night air.
I remember.
I remember our young love over the pay phone at the shopping center,
How I regaled you with details of my apartment.
It was just down the way only lacking a phone.
But there was no nearby apartment,
Only a lonely bench in the corner of the shopping center.
I remember.
I remember we decided to make a go of it down in the Pines,
Being as one, we sought to tackle a brave new world.
We were scared, nervous, excited.
I remember our quiet trip back to the hometown.
As I drove I felt anguish, sadness, dejection.
I remember.
I remember the two of us became the three of us.
Then we became four, and now we are five.
Though time has stretched beyond our union,
We have been blessed with three brilliant beams of light.
Their wit, their intellect, their loving kindness.
They remain the best part of me…
They remain the mooring lines that tether my loyalty to the hometown.

During the months following the official divorce, came the real "meltdown." I had molten hot lava spewing from my mouth at every turn. At work, I was simply off the chain. Everything presented a reason for me to snap. I was in a place of absolute desperation and The Lord had me right where He wanted me. He led me to Crossover Church on the last Sunday in December of 2015, and the stretching began. I remember thinking, "Man I'm all over the place. I need to get focused." During that first service I attended, the lead pastor informed the congregation that over the next few weeks we were going to be doing a series called "Focus." The first weeks of the new year would be spent dealing with focusing our lens to see God's vision for each of our lives. Huh, God had my attention from day one. I may be hard-headed, but I know His voice when I hear it.

My daughters also enjoyed the service, so we decided to make Crossover our new church home. After a few more weeks, I fell into some serious financial hard times. In February, I had to break my lease and move into a room for rent. I had pawned my TV and guitar some months earlier, and now I was losing my apartment. My entire life was being reduced into a single room. Furthermore, my daughters could no longer stay with me on weekends. This above all things hurt me the most. I was so stressed I couldn't see straight. Through the dense fog of despair, I did notice something interesting though. The street address on the house where I was moving was 2020. Yes, as in 20/20 vision. The Lord was speaking and I was now in a place to listen.

"Life doesn't always end with a sweet treat, but for some a fine cheese course of aged balance and satisfaction."

~NME

Chapter 9:
˜THE CHEESE COURSE˜

You may be wondering why the cheese course is at the end of the menu instead of the beginning. We typically think of having cheese as part of an hors d'oeuvres tray before a meal. This is true especially at an event that starts with a pre-meal mixer. However, on many high-end menus the chef will offer a cheese course in place of dessert, for those that prefer not to end the meal on such a decadent note. Even though I have a serious sweet tooth, I'm actually one of those people. If given the choice, I would probably choose the cheese course over dessert every time.

I call this part of my culinary career the cheese course because the things I learned and accomplished came with time. In the world of food preparation, few things take longer to perfect than cheese making. It is a craft comprised of both artistry and exact science. It requires passion, patience, skill, practice, routine, time, and more patience. You may also be wondering why I'm considering this season of my life as a part of my culinary career. After all, didn't I go to school and start another career in physical therapy? Actually, I still consider myself a chef, to the point that I continue to research food concepts and develop menu ideas. As a matter of fact, I learned how to make goat cheese during this season, long after I had stepped away from professional cooking.

I also have plans of using food to show God's love to the world around me. I'm not sure how it will play out, but I've known this entire time that at some point I'll come back to cooking on a professional level. Only this time it won't be in the same capacity, nor with the same objectives.

One of our pastors told us to ask ourselves this question; "Am I a person that works in a certain profession and happens to be a Christian, or am I a Christian who happens to work in a certain profession?" He then said, "However you answer that question, will dictate how you live your life." That very question has helped guide me in my ideas for future culinary endeavors. It has also guided me in writing this book to be honest.

I have wanted to write a book for about twenty years. What took so long you ask? Lack of focus. I had a complete lack of focus. All of those years, my motivation was based on just wanting to be a published author. Because I wasn't focused on what God wanted from me, my attention was everywhere. I never got anywhere with the actual writing process. Interestingly enough, living without my guitar and TV turned out to be a blessing. It gave me more opportunity to quiet my mind and get focused. You don't say! Maybe God really did know what He was doing after all.

I began writing everything that came to my mind. As the Lord gave it to me I wrote it down. I initially thought about putting together a book of poetry and other offerings. I'm still considering that, but for this assignment God soon began making the vision clearer. In late January of 2016 I had an idea for a book, but it had no form. It was just a collection of ideas. Bit by bit He showed me the vision and the format. Eventually it became clear. I would write a book about the life of a chef. But it wouldn't just deal with cooking. It would be from a Christian world view. It would deal with the spiritual, emotional, marital, and mental aspects of the life of a Christian who happened to cook for a living.

There were many nights that I thought, "Man, I'm glad I don't have my guitar or a TV because I would *not* be working right now." After only a few months of writing with supreme focus, voila! We had a book! Once I decided I was a Christian who happened to like writing, it completely opened up everything I didn't have the patience nor the peace of mind to write about before. In culinary terms, this book is a big block of twenty-year aged cheddar. Better still, *I'm* a big block of twenty-year aged cheddar. The Lord had been taking me through a strenuous process. Similarly, the process of making cheddar is quite rigorous. Here is the procedure as explained by the New England Cheese Making Supply Company:

•*Heat milk to 86F.*
•*Add 1 pack C-101 culture and let set for 45-60 min.*
•*Add 1/2 tsp rennet. let set 45 min @86F.*
•*Cut curds to 1/4-3/8"*

•*Then stir while slowly raising heat over 30 min to 102F. Maintain 102F and continue to stir for another 30 min more. Allow curds to settle under the whey for 20-30 min.*
•*Pour off whey and curds into a cloth lined colander. Place the colander and curds back into the empty pot and place the pot into a sink of 95-100F water to keep warm. Turn this curd mass at 15 min intervals for 2 hrs (at the 1 hr point cut the mass in half and stack the 2 halves). This is the CHEDDARING phase.*
•*Break this curd mass into 1/2-3/4" pieces*
•*Add salt (use 2% of the curd weight in salt). Add the salt in 3 phases allowing the salt to dissolve between additions. Stir often enough to keep from matting and this salting should take 30 min.*

•*Place cheese curds in cloth lined mold and press at 10 lbs for 15 min unwrap cheese from cloth, turn over, and re-wrap placing back in mold*

•*Press at the schedule below and unwrap, turn cheese and re-wrap between stages*

  ◦*12 lbs. for 30 min.*
  ◦*20 lbs. for 1 hr.*
  ◦*50 lbs. for 4 hrs.*
  ◦*50 lbs. again for another 24 hrs.*

NOTE: If the cheese has not consolidated well enough by this point, then increase time up to another 24 hrs. The weight can also be increased up to 100 lbs. if needed.

If still not consolidated the cheese curds were too dry so in the next batch do less stirring perhaps for less time. Also cutting the curds larger will make a moister cheese.

•*You may either Dry cheese for 1-3 days and wax OR you may follow my traditional bandaging as shown below.*

•*Age for 3-9 months depending on cheese moisture. The drier the cheese, the longer it can be aged.*

Yikes! Now that's an involved process. The thing about it is there is a lot of heating, adding culture, breaking, pressing and aging going on. Sounds like Christianity to me. Also, notice that with each round of pressing, the weight gets heavier and is applied for a longer period of time. Man, all these years I thought the weight was supposed to get lighter the more time I spent living this Christian life. Actually, I really did think that. There is a reason why Christ said, "My yoke is easy and my burden is light." He was reminding us to have a strength exchange with Him. We are to give Him our weakness, and take unto ourselves His strength. His yoke gives us a greater mechanical advantage to carry the weight of life. Now, I realize that though the load increases, it gets easier to bear as we trust His strength more and more. We are able to handle increasing loads with a decreased feeling of burden.

As with that block of cheddar, the truth of the matter is the firmer we become, and the more character we develop, the more time has been spent under heavier pressure. The cheese maker also states that if it doesn't come together, you can add more weight or more time to the pressing. Hmmm, sounds awfully familiar.

There are times however, when God will call for a break from the pressing. During one of my late-night writing sessions the Lord showed me how I had been that block of cheddar in His skillful hands. But to take me from raw ingredients to aged, refined product He was calling life to stop the press and allow me some rest. The resulting brain storm was an allegorical essay about a particular mad man…me! It was kind of funny the way the Lord was showing me to myself. It's almost like when you tell your kids about how they acted-up when they were younger. They usually just laugh and say something like, "Man, I can't believe I acted like that." My sentiments exactly! Here is that essay.

Road Rage

I heard a pastor on the radio yesterday preaching from Psalms 23 about Jehovah Rohi (God is my shepherd). He said that sometimes God will make you lie down and rest (…He makes me to lie down in green pastures). I have been feeling like the world is a day care center and I have been that tired and cranky little kid. Whiney to the point of throwing tantrums. I wasn't playing well with others. Every time I would attempt to use the blocks to build something, I would be mean to the other kids in the group if they didn't build it to my specs. Invariably someone would always place blocks contrary to my vision. Furthermore, I kept fighting and resisting nap time. To me it was an unfair punishment. I kept saying, "Father, it's not fair. Why do I keep having to take a nap? The other kids don't."

My life seemed like it was always going in this cycle leading back to the same place of despair, brokenness, and lack. It was like during the course of each "day" (season) I was always being brought back to this dreaded "nap time." NO matter how hard I worked and tried to get along with others, I always wound up being made to lie down and take a break. I didn't understand why. Why am I never getting ahead? Why can't I ever seem to make this life work for me? I felt like others who were younger than me weren't being called back for these routine naps. Why was I?

I was seeing things through carnal eyes. What I didn't understand was that spiritually these younger people were actually older than me. That epiphany was like an atom bomb to my spiritual ego. After all, I had been a deacon, led an outreach ministry for several years and prided myself on mobilizing for the needs of the people. The truth of the matter is that we all mature at different rates…it's not time-based.

Our pastor says, "There are no free passes." I was expecting to be of an older spiritual age just because of longevity. Boy, marriage sure took that theory and ripped it to shreds. After the failure of a twenty year marriage, I found I was still a spiritual minor in some ways. One of my problems has been poor self-image. I have continually compared myself to others. Even as a chef that just drove me into complete restlessness. I honestly never knew how insecure I really was. I was always strong in handling tough responsibilities, but never was confident in who I was on the inside. Spiritually this caused a cycling effect. I would walk with God for a while. Then as soon as I perceived someone else moving at a faster pace than me, I took my eyes off of God. I immediately would focus on others and what I thought they had that I didn't have. Then I attempted to chase those other people, who very well may have been following God's plans for their own lives. This would cause me to stop being led by God on my road to happiness. Instead, I became driven by wrong thinking down a path of self-destruction.

In December of 2015 this came to a boiling point. The facility where I was working had slowed down, so I decided to pick-up some extra work doing home health care. My plan was to take vacation from my full-time job while doing home health therapy. I would get paid for two jobs at one time. It was an excellent plan! The only problem was, it was "My" plan. I once again was burning the candle at both ends and leaving God out of the picture. At first I felt liberated because now I wasn't cooped-up inside all day. I was out driving around to all of my patients' homes. For the first time in a long time, I felt in control of my destination every day.

The huge problem was that the tires of my soul were getting worn down and very unbalanced. I didn't realize it, but my mind, will, and emotions were exhausted at this point. I had, only three months earlier, gone through a divorce from my best friend. My spiritual vehicle was in bad shape, but I didn't know it. In retrospect, I understand that the slowing down of work caseload at our facility was actually God saying to me, "Pull-over my son, get some rest. The day is wearing on you." I wasn't wanting to take a break…or rather, I couldn't. I had picked up the mantle that was reserved for Jehovah Rohi.

My understanding of being a Christian man meant driving hard, and refusing to stop until I saw the victory. Unfortunately, I was no longer in the driver's seat. I was actually in the passenger's seat and an idol was behind the wheel. The interesting thing is that this idol looked just like me. He was even wearing some old clothes of mine that I thought I had gotten rid of a long time ago. He was arrogant and brash. Spouting out all of these things on his ever important "to do" list. He was so busy ranting about all of the other drivers that he was weaving all over the road. This guy Arrogance was using terrible methodology performing what he called "aggressive driving techniques." I was being tossed and driven in one direction, and then in the opposite direction, as we went barreling down the road. He was constantly yelling and throwing his hands up. The other drivers were looking at him like, "Man, that guy needs to chill-out." As he went on and on I thought, "You idiot, don't you know those other drivers aren't even listening to you?! These people have bigger fish to fry than to be worried about driving the way you think they should." As a matter of fact, many of them had GPS devices on their dashboard directing them on which way to go. My man Arrogance was so full of righteous indignation (who are we kidding…down-right anger), that it was even starting to annoy me.

I was beginning to get so out of control that I was even losing patience with myself. I had gotten so impatient with everything and everyone around me, that the love of Christ just simply was not in me and most certainly wasn't coming out of me. The book of James 1:19,20 says, "Therefore my beloved brethren, let every man be swift to hear, slow to speak, slow to wrath. For the wrath of man does not produce the righteousness of God." The Lord was helping me to see that in all of my being right, I was completely wrong. I had become this road rage mad man that was letting everyone have it if they didn't meet my standards of excellence (which weren't even proper standards anyway).

Amid all of the fray while speeding down the highway, I happened to glance over my shoulder and noticed Jesus was sitting in the back seat. By this point my nerves were shot. I was spiritually, mentally, and physically spent. With a contrite heart, I implored Him, "Jesus, please take the wheel." I hung my head in shame. When I looked up again He was already in the driver's seat. I didn't know where Arrogance went, he was just gone. Jesus pulled the car over at a rest area and I thanked Him for saving me from that awful ride. I just didn't realize how tired I had become.

He looked at me and said, "John, this is a driver's education vehicle. You had a steering wheel and a brake pedal on your side of the car. You could have stopped at any time. Now be still, quiet your mind and take advantage of the time of rest I am providing for you."

As eye-opening as that scenario was, the healing process has still been long. Soon after the Lord showed me my behavior, I ended up having another crisis season. It was really starting to take a toll on my will to continue on. I was growing tired of going through these seasons of spiritual, mental, and emotional turmoil. They had also gotten more frequent since the divorce. I started to really want some answers. Why was this happening? Why was life so difficult to navigate? Why did I continue to find it so hard to just be social with people?

Eventually, I sought help. I got two assessments done by certified counselors. It turns out that they believe I'm Manic Depressive. That boss of mine, so many years earlier, was actually on to something. Boy, talk about life coming full circle. I really debated for a long time about whether to include this part of my story in the book. It's very humbling to even speak about. I asked God and ultimately I felt led to include it for one major reason. It is the kind of issue that so many people in the Church feel unable to discuss with anyone. Sometimes we tend to over "religiousize" things like this.

When I began suspecting that I might be Manic Depressive some time back, I mentioned it to a Christian acquaintance of mine. Her response was, "John, don't believe the lies of the enemy." She had no other words to offer. I found it interesting, because if I had said that I thought my arm was broken, that wouldn't have been the response. If a woman were to tell me she was diagnosed with breast cancer, my response better not be to blow it off by saying, "Oh, don't believe the lies of the enemy." I understand biblical truth. The circumstance may say Manic Depression, but the truth is I have victory over it in Jesus' name. But we can't fight against an enemy that we don't acknowledge. It has helped me understand not only *what* to fight, but also *where* it's coming from. Ultimately, I was never formally diagnosed with anything at all, but I am more aware of what may be some of the cause of my struggles.

I had a recent conversation with a coworker who is Christian and has battled with clinical anxiety. He said something very profound; "Don't try to fight the behavior, you'll lose every time. You need to find out the root cause, and go from there." Now that sounds like proper Christian counsel to me. Christ came so that we would have life more abundantly, not live more religiously. May we pray and fight for one another on all fronts, no matter where strongholds may lie.

Whatever the root cause, my life always seemed to me like it was going in circles. Not the good kind of circles, like driving on the beltway and feeling freedom to enter and exit at will, while learning our way around. No, these have been circles that seemed to zap the spiritual energy out of me. Any formal medical diagnosis aside, I have since learned that a major reason for my perpetual circling has to do with unbelief.

The Children of Israel wandered in the wilderness for forty years while in search of the Promised Land. God allowed this because they had doubted Him. They even accused Moses of dealing dishonestly with them. They asked why he had brought them out of Egypt that they may die in the wilderness. According to them, they were better off staying in bondage to the Egyptians. Along with their grumbling about the current conditions, they were also immobilized by fear. Twelve men had been sent out to spy the Promised Land. When they returned, ten of them gave the report that the land flowed with milk and honey, but that it was inhabited by giants.

Two, however, gave the testimony that this was the land God had given them, if they would just not be afraid. Despite Joshua and Caleb's optimism, the people were nonetheless stricken with fear. God said that that entire generation of unbelief would pass away and not see the Promised Land.

I am just beginning to realize that all these years I've been sabotaging my own growth and success because of unbelief. Subconsciously, I didn't think I was worthy of having anything good. I still wrestle with feeling awkward sometimes if I get blessed with something nice. I feel like I don't deserve it. Lisa even pointed out to me one time years ago that I seemed to relate to the underdog. To this day, whenever I go anywhere to eat I like to watch the kitchen staff whenever possible. No matter how far up the ladder I climb, I still relate to the lowly cook "slinging hash" in the kitchen. Our pastor's words keep ringing in my ears, "However you see yourself is how you'll live your life."

Focusing on God is helping me see myself differently. Joining Crossover Church has actually been a sort of coming full circle for me. The church is located on Fowler Avenue in of course, suitcase city! It's literally about an eight-minute walk from the apartment I had over twenty years ago, just before Lisa and I got married. The building Crossover is in was a Toys 'R Us store back then. Boy, so much has changed, yet so much has stayed the same. I have spent my whole life since the age of sixteen trying to get out of Tampa. I've spent twenty-two years trying to escape suitcase city. Clearly, God has other plans, because I keep finding my way back.

Throughout all of these years of running, God has consistently placed a particular ministry on my heart. I found that I really relate to troubled youth. Whenever I meet struggling teens, I just want to pour all of the love of Christ into their soul. It would be just like God to bring me back to the place of my desperate past to catapult me into my future.

Up until very recently, I have continued to wrestle with feeling inadequate in terms of stepping out into ministry. During a recent mid-week service, one of our pastors posed the simple question, "Who's report will you believe?" It was a reminder to me that there has been a Joshua and Caleb within me patiently holding on to the promises of God all these years. It's time to follow God's plans for my life and claim the territory He showed me so many years ago. As I resolve to step into my destiny I pray that you would pursue *your* calling with all diligence. That being said, I leave you with what has become one of my favorite verses in any song I've ever heard. It encapsulates every experience this meal of a lifetime has provided me. All of the struggles, failures, and triumphs. Yet, it shines the beacon of hope that nourishment may come from life's next meal. Bon appetit!

Look at history, rebuilding always starts with yielding.
Started with Nehemiah on his knees kneeling.
Praying and fasting, hands to the ceiling,
The Master of the universe started revealing.
The master plan,
He stepped up, he could have ran...
I'm a fan,
Of his courageous obedience.
This is one of the key missing rebuilding ingredients.
That can get polluted by what the culture's feeding us.
That's how the enemy is beating us and leading us,
Into lives that crumble, churches that stumble, a world that fumbles.
Brings us full circle back to humble.
Humble beginnings to re-heal,
Humble hearts to re-yield,
Now humble beast go and rebuild.

Tommy Kyllonen

151

Epilogue

*"The heat of pressure,
is no comparison to the anguish of regret,
therefore continue faithfully,
eventually inevitability will have its way,
bringing all circumstances into subjection,
causing that which will be
to become that which is."*

~J.S.E./ *NME*

55158021R00084

Made in the USA
Middletown, DE
15 July 2019